Miracle Whip
COOKBOOK

PUBLICATIONS INTERNATIONAL, LTD.

Miracle Whip
COOKBOOK

Introduction	**3**
Cold Appetizers	**4**
Hot Appetizers	**12**
Fruit & Vegetable Salads	**24**
Potato & Pasta Salads	**40**
Main-Dish Salads	**48**
Entrees	**56**
Side Dishes	**78**
Index	**94**

Copyright © 1989 Kraft, Inc.
All rights reserved.

MIRACLE WHIP, KRAFT, CASINO, PHILADELPHIA BRAND, PARKAY, VELVEETA, SAUCEWORKS, and LENDER'S are registered trademarks of Kraft, Inc., Glenview, IL 60025.

PILLSBURY is a registered trademark of The Pillsbury Co., Minneapolis, MN 55402.

Recipe development by the Kraft Kitchens.

Produced by Publications International, Ltd., Lincolnwood, Illinois.

Pictured on front cover (clockwise from top left): Southwestern Appetizer Torte (see page 9), Potpourri Fruit Bowl (see page 26), Tasty Turkey Pot Pie (see page 64) and Stuffed Pasta Shells (see page 72).

ISBN 0-88176-699-2

Manufactured in Yugoslavia.

h g f e d c b a

Introduction

The trend in today's cooking is toward recipes that are not only fast and easy to prepare but also nutritious and great tasting. With this in mind, the Kraft Kitchens have developed 108 delicious recipes and are bringing them to you in this book.

Each of these recipes has been tested and retested to make sure you will be satisfied with each one you try. You will love the creative entertaining ideas as well as the simple, down-to-earth, family recipes that are included. Paging through this book gives you an idea of all the incredible dishes that you can prepare using versatile Miracle Whip salad dressing. These recipes are designed for almost every need and occasion: for young and old, families and singles, two-career households, and dinner and holiday guests.

The blend of select ingredients in Miracle Whip salad dressing gives it a tangy zip that enhances the taste of each and every one of these delicious recipes. Miracle Whip salad dressing, which was originally thought of as only an ingredient for salads or as a spread for sandwiches, has become an accepted ingredient for cooking, suitable for many recipes. Miracle Whip salad dressing can even be substituted for mayonnaise in any recipe to make it more special. Today, Miracle Whip salad dressing is an indispensable ingredient used by families everywhere.

Also, the great taste of Miracle Whip salad dressing makes sense from a health standpoint. Miracle Whip salad dressing has 36% less fat and 30% fewer calories than mayonnaise. And it's low in cholesterol. Miracle Whip cholesterol free dressing is just as low in fat and calories as regular Miracle Whip salad dressing and has *no* cholesterol. For the especially health conscious, Miracle Whip *Light* reduced calorie salad dressing with no cholesterol has 42% less fat with 30% fewer calories than regular Miracle

Whip salad dressing. What's more, all three dressings may be interchanged in recipes to suit your diet requirements. Enjoy the tangy zip of Miracle Whip salad dressing in these delicious recipes and cook with the great taste that makes sense.

A Word About the Timings for the Recipes

To aid you in organizing your meals, each recipe gives a preparation time and may give a baking, cooking or broiling time. All times are rounded up to the nearest 5 minutes. The preparation times are based on the amount of time required to assemble the recipe before baking, cooking, chilling, freezing or serving. These times include preparation steps, such as chopping, mixing, cooking rice, pasta, vegetables, etc. If an ingredient can be purchased prepared, such as cooked chicken from a deli, the preparation time will not include the time it takes to prepare that particular food item. The baking, cooking or broiling times are based on the maximum cooking times plus any standing times.

Many of the recipes in this book give microwave directions. Since microwave ovens vary in wattage, our home economists test recipes in standard household microwave ovens measuring 500, 600 and 700 watts. Cooking times should be used as a guideline—check for doneness before increasing the cooking times. Lower wattage microwave ovens may require longer cooking times. Cooking times may also vary as a result of food temperatures, shapes and weight.

Cold Appetizers

Entertaining is made easy with this wonderful variety of dips, spreads and finger foods. Many of these special treats can be whipped up in less than 15 minutes and are great for family snacking. Pictured here is Pesto-Layered Spread; see page 6 for recipe.

Pesto-Layered Spread

    1 envelope unflavored gelatin
  ¼ cup cold water
  ½ cup MIRACLE WHIP Salad
      Dressing
    1 8-oz. pkg. PHILADELPHIA
      BRAND Cream Cheese,
      softened
    2 tablespoons fresh prepared
      pesto
  ½ cup chopped walnuts, toasted

Combine gelatin and water in small saucepan; let stand 1 minute. Stir over low heat until dissolved; cool slightly. Gradually add gelatin to salad dressing, mixing until well blended. Reserve 2 tablespoons gelatin mixture; gradually add remaining gelatin mixture to cream cheese, mixing until well blended. Combine reserved gelatin mixture and pesto; mix well. Layer one-third cream cheese mixture in lightly oiled 5½×3-inch loaf pan or 2-cup mold; cover with half of pesto mixture. Repeat layers, ending with cream cheese layer. Sprinkle with walnuts; press lightly into cream cheese mixture. Chill until firm. Unmold onto serving plate. Serve with toasted French bread slices. Makes 1½ cups.

Preparation time: 15 minutes plus chilling

Variation: Substitute 2-cup bowl for loaf pan; do not unmold.

Recipe tip: For easy removal of spread, line loaf pan or mold with plastic wrap before filling.

Creamy Spinach Dip

    1 10-oz. pkg. frozen chopped
      spinach, thawed, well
      drained
    1 cup MIRACLE WHIP Salad
      Dressing
    1 cup sour cream
  ½ cup chopped parsley
  ¼ cup green onion slices
    1 teaspoon dill weed
  ½ teaspoon lemon pepper

Combine ingredients; mix well. Cover; chill. Serve with assorted vegetable dippers. Makes 2½ cups.

Preparation time: 10 minutes plus chilling

Variations: Substitute plain yogurt for sour cream.

Substitute MIRACLE WHIP Light Reduced Calorie Salad Dressing with no cholesterol for Regular Salad Dressing.

Guacamole Dip

    1 ripe avocado, peeled, mashed
  ½ cup chopped tomato
  ¼ cup MIRACLE WHIP Salad
      Dressing
    2 tablespoons chopped onion
  ¼ teaspoon salt
      Dash of hot pepper sauce
    2 crisply cooked bacon slices,
      crumbled

Combine ingredients except bacon; mix well. Stir in bacon just before serving. Serve with tortilla chips. Makes 1½ cups.

Preparation time: 15 minutes

Creamy Spinach Dip

Southwestern Appetizer Torte

    4 8- to 10-inch flour tortillas
    1 ripe avocado, peeled, mashed
    ½ cup MIRACLE WHIP Salad
        Dressing
    ¼ cup green onion slices
    ¼ teaspoon garlic powder
    1 15-oz. can black beans, drained
    1 cup chopped tomatoes
        (optional)
    ½ cup chunky salsa
    1 4-oz. can chopped green
        chilies, drained
    ½ cup (2 ozs.) 100% Natural
        KRAFT Shredded Sharp
        Cheddar Cheese

Soften tortillas as directed on package. Combine avocado, ¼ cup salad dressing, 2 tablespoons onions and garlic powder; mix well. Place one tortilla on serving plate; cover with beans and second tortilla. Top with avocado mixture, third tortilla, tomatoes, salsa and last tortilla. Cover with combined remaining salad dressing and chilies. Sprinkle with cheese and remaining onions. Makes 10 servings.

Preparation time: 20 minutes

Creamy Dill Dip

    1 cup MIRACLE WHIP Light
        Reduced Calorie Salad
        Dressing with no cholesterol
    2 tablespoons finely chopped
        onion
    1 tablespoon milk
    1 teaspoon dill weed

Combine ingredients; mix well. Cover; chill. Serve with vegetable dippers. Makes 1 cup.

Preparation time: 5 minutes plus chilling

Variation: Substitute 1 tablespoon chopped fresh dill for 1 teaspoon dill weed.

Vegetable Pizza

    1 8-oz. can PILLSBURY
        Refrigerated Quick Crescent
        Dinner Rolls
    1 8-oz. pkg. PHILADELPHIA
        BRAND Cream Cheese,
        softened
    ½ cup MIRACLE WHIP Salad
        Dressing
    ½ teaspoon Italian seasoning
    ¾ cup chopped red pepper
    ¾ cup chopped radishes
    ½ cup pitted ripe olive slices
    2 tablespoons green onion slices
    ½ cup (2 ozs.) 100% Natural
        KRAFT Shredded Sharp
        Cheddar Cheese

Unroll dough into two rectangles. Place in 13×9-inch baking pan. Press onto bottom and ¼ inch up sides of pan to form crust. Seal perforations. Bake at 375°, 10 minutes. Cool. Combine cream cheese, salad dressing and seasoning; mix well. Spread over crust. Top with remaining ingredients. Cover; chill. Cut into squares to serve. Makes approximately 2 dozen.

Preparation time: 20 minutes plus chilling

Southwestern Appetizer Torte

Shrimp Spread

1 8-oz. pkg. PHILADELPHIA
    BRAND Cream Cheese,
    softened
½ cup MIRACLE WHIP Salad
    Dressing
1 4¼-oz. can tiny cocktail
    shrimp, drained, rinsed
⅓ cup finely chopped onion
⅛ teaspoon garlic salt

Combine cream cheese and salad
dressing, mixing until well
blended. Stir in remaining
ingredients. Cover; chill. Serve
with assorted crackers. Makes 2
cups.

Preparation time: 10 minutes plus
chilling

Vegetable-Laced Bagelettes

1 cup shredded carrots
1 cup shredded zucchini
2 hard-cooked eggs, finely
    chopped
¼ cup MIRACLE WHIP Salad
    Dressing
½ teaspoon salt
¼ teaspoon pepper
10 LENDER'S Pre-Sliced Frozen
    Plain Bagelettes, toasted
1 cup alfalfa sprouts

Combine ingredients except
bagelettes and sprouts; mix lightly.
Top bagelette halves with sprouts
and vegetable mixture. Makes 20
appetizers.

Preparation time: 35 minutes

Variation: Substitute MIRACLE
WHIP Light Reduced Calorie Salad
Dressing with no cholesterol for
Regular Salad Dressing.

Munching Onion Dip

1 8-oz. pkg. PHILADELPHIA
    BRAND Cream Cheese,
    softened
½ cup MIRACLE WHIP Salad
    Dressing
¼ cup milk
⅓ cup green onion slices
1 teaspoon Worcestershire sauce

Combine cream cheese, salad
dressing and milk, mixing until
well blended. Stir in remaining
ingredients. Cover; chill. Serve
with potato chips. Makes 2 cups.

Preparation time: 10 minutes plus
chilling

Variation: Add one garlic clove,
minced.

Smooth Cheddar Spread

2 cups (8 ozs.) 100% Natural
    KRAFT Shredded Sharp
    Cheddar Cheese
⅓ cup MIRACLE WHIP Salad
    Dressing
2 tablespoons green onion slices
½ teaspoon Worcestershire sauce

Place cheese and salad dressing in
food processor work bowl; process
until smooth. Add onions and
Worcestershire sauce; process 1
minute. Chill. Serve with assorted
crackers. Makes 1½ cups.

Preparation time: 5 minutes plus
chilling

Variation: Substitute electric mixer
for food processor; mix at medium
speed until well blended.

Shrimp Spread

Hot Appetizers

Impress family and guests with the delectable treats that follow. Use them as great nibbles for party snacks or as a prelude to whet appetites for the main course. Pictured here is Sombrero Appetizer; see page 14 for recipe.

Sombrero Appetizer

1 lb. ground beef
½ lb. VELVEETA Mexican Pasteurized Process Cheese Spread with Jalapeño Pepper, cubed
⅔ cup MIRACLE WHIP Salad Dressing
¼ cup chopped onion

Brown meat; drain. Add remaining ingredients; mix lightly. Spoon mixture into 9-inch pie plate. Bake at 350°, 10 minutes; stir. Continue baking 5 minutes. Top with chopped tomatoes, pitted ripe olive slices and jalapeño pepper, if desired. Serve with tortilla or corn chips. Makes 4½ cups.

Preparation time: 15 minutes

Baking time: 15 minutes

MICROWAVE: Crumble meat into 1½-quart microwave-safe casserole. Microwave on High 4 to 5 minutes or until meat loses pink color, stirring every 2 minutes; drain. Stir in remaining ingredients. Spoon mixture into 9-inch microwave-safe pie plate. Microwave on High 3 minutes or until thoroughly heated, stirring after 2 minutes. Stir. Top with chopped tomatoes, pitted ripe olive slices and jalapeño pepper, if desired. Serve with tortilla or corn chips.

Cheesy Crab Squares

2 8-oz. cans PILLSBURY Refrigerated Quick Crescent Dinner Rolls
½ cup MIRACLE WHIP Salad Dressing
2 teaspoons lemon juice
⅛ teaspoon pepper
2 cups (8 ozs.) 100% Natural KRAFT Shredded Sharp Cheddar Cheese
6 ozs. imitation crabmeat, chopped
⅓ cup green onion slices
1 tablespoon chopped parsley

Unroll dough into four rectangles. Place in 15×10×1-inch jelly roll pan; press onto bottom and halfway up sides of pan to form crust. Seal perforations. Bake at 375°, 10 minutes. Combine salad dressing, juice and pepper; mix well. Add cheese, crabmeat, onions and parsley; mix lightly. Spread over crust. Continue baking 12 to 15 minutes or until cheese is melted. Let stand 5 minutes; cut into squares. Makes approximately 2 dozen appetizers.

Preparation time: 15 minutes

Baking time: 15 minutes plus standing

Make ahead: Prepare crust as directed; cool. Cover tightly. Combine crabmeat mixture as directed. Cover; chill. Spread crabmeat mixture over crust just before baking. Bake at 350°, 15 minutes or until cheese is melted.

Cheesy Crab Squares

Party Chicken Sandwiches

1½ cups finely chopped cooked chicken
1 cup MIRACLE WHIP Salad Dressing
1 4-oz. can chopped green chilies, drained
¾ cup (3 ozs.) 100% Natural KRAFT Shredded Sharp Cheddar Cheese
¼ cup finely chopped onion
36 party rye or pumpernickel bread slices

Combine chicken, salad dressing, chilies, cheese and onions; mix lightly. Cover bread with chicken mixture. Broil 5 minutes or until lightly browned. Serve hot. Garnish as desired. Makes 3 dozen.

Preparation time: 15 minutes

Broiling time: 5 minutes

Variation: Substitute MIRACLE WHIP Light Reduced Calorie Salad Dressing with no cholesterol for Regular Salad Dressing.

Hot Swiss and Almond Spread

1 8-oz. pkg. PHILADELPHIA BRAND Cream Cheese, softened
⅓ cup MIRACLE WHIP Salad Dressing
1½ cups (6 ozs.) shredded 100% Natural KRAFT Swiss Cheese
⅓ cup sliced almonds, toasted
2 tablespoons green onion slices
⅛ teaspoon ground nutmeg
⅛ teaspoon pepper

Combine cream cheese and salad dressing, mixing until well blended. Stir in remaining ingredients. Spread mixture into 9-inch pie plate. Bake at 350°, 15 minutes, stirring after 8 minutes. Garnish with additional toasted sliced almonds, if desired. Serve with assorted crackers or party rye bread slices. Makes 2⅓ cups.

Preparation time: 15 minutes

Baking time: 15 minutes

MICROWAVE: Using 9-inch microwave-safe pie plate, prepare recipe as directed except for baking. Microwave on Medium (50%) 6 minutes or until cheese is melted and mixture is warm, stirring after 4 minutes. (Do not overcook.) Stir before serving. Garnish and serve as directed.

Microwave tips: To soften cream cheese, microwave in microwave-safe bowl on Medium (50%) 30 seconds.

To toast almonds, microwave 1 teaspoon PARKAY Margarine in 9-inch microwave-safe pie plate on High 30 seconds or until melted. Add ½ cup sliced almonds; toss lightly. Microwave on High 6 to 8 minutes or until lightly browned, stirring every 2 minutes. Let stand 5 minutes. Reserve 3 tablespoons almonds for garnish.

Party Chicken Sandwiches

Creamy Egg Rolls

1 14-oz. can chop suey
    vegetables, chopped, well
    drained
1 cup chopped imitation
    crabmeat
1/4 cup MIRACLE WHIP Salad
    Dressing
2 teaspoons soy sauce
8 egg roll wrappers
    Oil
    Mustard Sauce (recipe follows)
    Apricot Sauce (recipe follows)

Combine vegetables, crabmeat, salad dressing and soy sauce; mix lightly. For each egg roll, spoon approximately 1/4 cup crabmeat mixture onto center of each wrapper; moisten edges of wrapper with water. Fold one corner over filling; fold opposite corners over first fold. Roll remaining corner over to seal. Fry, in batches, in 1-inch hot oil, 375°, 2 to 3 minutes or until golden brown on all sides, turning once. Drain on paper towels. Prepare Mustard Sauce and Apricot Sauce. Serve with egg rolls. Makes 8 servings.

Mustard Sauce

1/4 cup MIRACLE WHIP Salad
    Dressing
1 tablespoon dijon mustard

Combine ingredients; mix well. Makes 1/4 cup.

Apricot Sauce

1/4 cup MIRACLE WHIP Salad
    Dressing
2 tablespoons KRAFT Apricot
    Preserves

Combine ingredients; mix well. Makes 1/3 cup.

Preparation time: 15 minutes

Cooking time: 10 minutes

Recipe tip: For a more blended flavor, prepare sauces ahead of time. Cover; chill.

Turkey Empanadas

2 cups finely chopped cooked
    turkey or chicken
1/2 cup MIRACLE WHIP Salad
    Dressing
1/2 cup (2 ozs.) 100% Natural
    KRAFT Shredded Sharp
    Cheddar Cheese
2 tablespoons green onion slices
1/8 teaspoon pepper
1 17 1/4-oz. pkg. frozen puff
    pastry, thawed

Combine turkey, salad dressing, cheese, onions and pepper; mix lightly. On lightly floured surface, roll one pastry sheet to 12-inch square. Cut into nine 4-inch squares. Spoon approximately 2 tablespoons filling onto center of each square. Fold diagonally in half; press edges together with fork to seal. Repeat with remaining pastry and filling. Place on ungreased cookie sheet. Bake at 450°, 12 to 15 minutes or until golden brown. Makes 18 appetizers.

Preparation time: 35 minutes

Baking time: 15 minutes

*Creamy Egg Rolls with Mustard
Sauce and Apricot Sauce*

Artichoke Appetizers

2 8-oz. cans PILLSBURY Refrigerated Quick Crescent Dinner Rolls
¾ cup (3 ozs.) 100% Natural KRAFT Shredded Low Moisture Part-Skim Mozzarella Cheese
¾ cup (3 ozs.) KRAFT 100% Grated Parmesan Cheese
½ cup MIRACLE WHIP Salad Dressing
1 15-oz. can artichoke hearts, drained, finely chopped
1 4-oz. can chopped green chilies, drained (optional)

Unroll dough into four rectangles. Place in 15×10×1-inch jelly roll pan; press onto bottom and halfway up sides of pan to form crust. Seal perforations. Bake at 375°, 10 minutes. Combine remaining ingredients; mix well. Spread over crust. Bake at 375°, 15 minutes or until cheese is melted. Let stand 5 minutes; cut to serve. Garnish with thin red pepper strips and parsley, if desired. Makes approximately 3 dozen.

Preparation time: 15 minutes

Baking time: 15 minutes plus standing

Garden Vegetable Party Pitas

2 pita bread rounds, cut in half
1 cup (4 ozs.) shredded CASINO Brand Natural Monterey Jack Cheese
⅓ cup MIRACLE WHIP Salad Dressing
¼ cup chopped radishes
¼ cup green onion slices

Cut each bread half into four triangles; split triangles in half. Place on cookie sheet. Bake at 425°, 5 minutes or until edges are lightly toasted. Combine remaining ingredients; mix lightly. Spread onto bread; continue baking 5 minutes or until cheese is melted. Makes 32 appetizers.

Preparation time: 10 minutes

Baking time: 5 minutes

Variations: Substitute MIRACLE WHIP Light Reduced Calorie Salad Dressing with no cholesterol for Regular Salad Dressing.

Substitute 100% Natural KRAFT Swiss Cheese for CASINO Brand Natural Monterey Jack Cheese.

Substitute 24 party rye or pumpernickel bread slices for pita bread rounds. Place on cookie sheet. Continue baking as directed.

Artichoke Appetizers

Garden Appetizers

4 cups shredded zucchini
2 cups shredded carrots
½ cup flour
¾ cup MIRACLE WHIP Salad
    Dressing
1 cup (4 ozs.) shredded CASINO
    Brand Natural Monterey Jack
    Cheese
½ cup (2 ozs.) KRAFT 100%
    Grated Parmesan Cheese
¼ cup chopped onion
1 teaspoon dried basil leaves,
    crushed
    Dash of pepper
4 eggs, beaten

Combine zucchini, carrots and flour; toss lightly. Add salad dressing, cheeses, onions, basil and pepper; mix well. Blend in eggs. Spread mixture into lightly greased 13×9-inch baking pan. Bake at 375°, 30 to 35 minutes or until set. Cool slightly; cut into squares. Makes approximately 4 dozen.

Preparation time: 15 minutes

Baking time: 35 minutes plus cooling

Baked Potato Spears

3 large baking potatoes
¼ cup MIRACLE WHIP Light
    Reduced Calorie Salad
    Dressing with no cholesterol
    Onion salt
    Pepper
    Parma Dip (recipe follows)
    Hearty Barbecue Dip (recipe
    follows)

Cut potatoes lengthwise into wedges. Brush with salad dressing. Season with onion salt and pepper. Place on greased 15×10×1-inch jelly roll pan. Bake at 375°, 50 minutes or until tender and golden brown. Prepare Parma Dip and Hearty Barbecue Dip. Serve with potatoes. Makes 4 servings.

Parma Dip

1 cup MIRACLE WHIP Light
    Reduced Calorie Salad
    Dressing with no cholesterol
¼ cup (1 oz.) KRAFT 100%
    Grated Parmesan Cheese
¼ cup milk
1 tablespoon chopped chives

Combine ingredients; mix well. Makes 1¼ cups.

Hearty Barbecue Dip

½ cup MIRACLE WHIP Light
    Reduced Calorie Salad
    Dressing with no cholesterol
¼ cup KRAFT Thick 'n Spicy
    Barbecue Sauce with Honey
2 tablespoons chopped onion
2 tablespoons chopped green
    pepper

Combine ingredients; mix well. Makes 1 cup.

Preparation time: 10 minutes

Baking time: 50 minutes

Recipe tip: For a more blended flavor, prepare dips ahead of time. Cover; chill.

Baked Potato Spears with Parma Dip and Hearty Barbecue Dip

Fruit & Vegetable Salads

The recipes in this chapter are sure to create renewed enthusiasm for salads with your family. Fresh ingredients are the base for most of these colorful side-dish salads. Pictured here is Wild Rice & Pepper Salad; see page 26 for recipe.

Wild Rice & Pepper Salad

    1 6-oz. pkg. long-grain & wild rice
    1/2 cup MIRACLE WHIP Salad Dressing
    2 tablespoons olive oil
    1/2 teaspoon black pepper
    1/4 teaspoon grated lemon peel
    1 cup chopped red pepper
    1 cup chopped yellow pepper
    1/4 cup 1-inch green onion pieces

Prepare rice as directed on package, omitting margarine. Cool. Combine salad dressing, oil, black pepper and peel; mix well. Add remaining ingredients; mix lightly. Serve at room temperature or chilled. Makes 6 servings.

Preparation time: 35 minutes

Variation: Substitute MIRACLE WHIP Light Reduced Calorie Salad Dressing with no cholesterol for Regular Salad Dressing.

Blue Cheese Salad

    1 head iceberg lettuce
    3/4 cup MIRACLE WHIP Salad Dressing
    1 4-oz. pkg. KRAFT Chopped Blue Cheese Crumbles

Cut lettuce into four slices. For each serving, spread lettuce with salad dressing. Sprinkle with cheese. Makes 4 servings.

Preparation time: 5 minutes

Potpourri Fruit Bowl

    1/4 cup MIRACLE WHIP Salad Dressing
    1/4 cup sour cream
    3 tablespoons KRAFT Apricot Preserves
    1 tablespoon lemon juice
    2 cups cantaloupe balls
    1 peach, sliced
    1 cup strawberry halves
    1 cup grapes

Combine salad dressing, sour cream, preserves and juice; mix well. Cover; chill. Combine fruit; mix lightly. Serve with salad dressing mixture. Makes 4 servings.

Preparation time: 20 minutes plus chilling

Variations: Prepare salad dressing mixture as directed. Cut one cantaloupe in half horizontally; remove seeds. Scoop out melon balls, leaving shells intact. Combine fruit; mix lightly. Cut edge of shells in zig zag design, if desired. Fill with fruit mixture. Serve with salad dressing mixture.

Substitute MIRACLE WHIP Light Reduced Calorie Salad Dressing with no cholesterol for Regular Salad Dressing and plain yogurt for sour cream.

Potpourri Fruit Bowl

Zippy Bean Salad

1/2 cup MIRACLE WHIP Salad
    Dressing
1 16-oz. can kidney beans,
    drained, rinsed
1 9-oz. pkg. frozen cut green
    beans, thawed, drained
1/2 cup celery slices
1/2 cup onion rings
2 tablespoons vinegar
    Few drops hot pepper sauce
    Salt and black pepper
4 crisply cooked bacon slices,
    crumbled

Combine salad dressing, beans, celery, onions, vinegar and hot pepper sauce; mix lightly. Season with salt and black pepper to taste. Cover; chill. Add bacon just before serving. Makes 6 to 8 servings.

Preparation time: 15 minutes plus chilling

Variations: Omit vinegar. Substitute two 15-oz. cans bean salad, drained, for kidney beans and green beans.

Substitute MIRACLE WHIP Light Reduced Calorie Salad Dressing with no cholesterol for Regular Salad Dressing.

Our Basic Waldorf Salad

1/2 cup MIRACLE WHIP Salad
    Dressing
1/8 teaspoon ground cinnamon
2 cups chopped apple
1 cup KRAFT Miniature
    Marshmallows
3/4 cup thin celery slices
1/4 cup chopped walnuts, toasted

Combine salad dressing and cinnamon; mix well. Add remaining ingredients except walnuts; mix lightly. Cover; chill. Add walnuts just before serving. Makes 4 to 6 servings.

Preparation time: 10 minutes plus chilling

Variations: Add 8 1/4-oz. can pineapple chunks, drained.

Add 1 cup raisins, dates or seedless grapes.

Add 2 cups chopped cooked chicken, turkey or ham.

Carrot Salad

2 cups shredded carrots
2 cups chopped apples
1/2 cup MIRACLE WHIP Salad
    Dressing
1/2 cup raisins
1/2 cup chopped pecans

Combine ingredients; mix lightly. Makes 6 servings.

Preparation time: 15 minutes

Variation: Substitute MIRACLE WHIP Light Reduced Calorie Salad Dressing with no cholesterol for Regular Salad Dressing.

Food processor tip: To shred carrots, use shredding disk of food processor.

Zippy Bean Salad

Piña Colada Freeze

1 large ripe banana, mashed
1 20-oz. can crushed pineapple, drained
⅔ cup MIRACLE WHIP Salad Dressing
⅔ cup cream of coconut
2 cups thawed frozen whipped topping

Combine banana, pineapple, salad dressing and cream of coconut; mix well. Fold in whipped topping. Spoon mixture into 9×5-inch loaf pan; cover. Freeze until firm. Remove from freezer and place in refrigerator 30 minutes before serving. Spoon or scoop into serving dishes. Sprinkle with toasted flaked coconut, if desired. Garnish with fresh fruit. Makes 12 servings.

Preparation time: 10 minutes plus freezing

Variation: Add ¼ cup rum.

Crunchy Pea Salad

½ cup MIRACLE WHIP Salad Dressing
¼ cup KRAFT "Zesty" Italian Dressing
1 10-oz. pkg. frozen peas, thawed, drained
1 cup chopped celery
1 cup peanuts
¼ cup chopped red onion
6 crisply cooked bacon slices, crumbled

Combine dressings; mix well. Add remaining ingredients except bacon; mix lightly. Cover; chill. Add bacon just before serving; mix lightly. Makes 6 to 8 servings.

Preparation time: 15 minutes

Variation: Serve in tomatoes, cut into six wedges almost to stem end.

Cranberry Waldorf Fluff

1½ cups cranberries, finely chopped
1 cup KRAFT Miniature Marshmallows
¼ cup sugar
1½ cups finely chopped apple
½ cup MIRACLE WHIP Salad Dressing
¼ cup chopped walnuts
⅛ teaspoon ground cinnamon

Combine cranberries, miniature marshmallows and sugar; mix lightly. Cover; chill. Add remaining ingredients; mix lightly. Makes 6 servings.

Preparation time: 20 minutes plus chilling

Piña Colada Freeze

Walnut-Grape Salad

½ cup MIRACLE WHIP Salad
    Dressing
2 tablespoons KRAFT Orange
    Marmalade
2 cups seedless red grapes
1 cup seedless green grapes
1 cup celery slices
¾ cup chopped walnuts, toasted

Combine salad dressing and marmalade, mixing until well blended. Add grapes and celery; mix lightly. Cover; chill. Stir in walnuts just before serving. Makes 4½ cups.

Preparation time: 15 minutes plus chilling

Variations: For main-dish salad, add 2 cups chopped ham.

Substitute MIRACLE WHIP Light Reduced Calorie Salad Dressing with no cholesterol for Regular Salad Dressing.

BLT Salad Toss

1½ qts. torn lettuce
1 cup cherry tomato halves
½ cup chopped green pepper
6 crisply cooked bacon slices,
    crumbled
½ cup red onion rings
1 cup MIRACLE WHIP Salad
    Dressing
½ cup (2 ozs.) 100% Natural
    KRAFT Shredded Sharp
    Cheddar Cheese

In 2-quart serving bowl, layer lettuce, tomatoes, peppers, bacon and onions. Cover with salad dressing, spreading to edges of bowl to seal. Sprinkle with cheese. Cover; chill. Toss lightly just before serving. Makes 4 to 6 servings.

Preparation time: 15 minutes plus chilling

Variations: Substitute MIRACLE WHIP Light Reduced Calorie Salad Dressing with no cholesterol for Regular Salad Dressing.

Sun-Sational Lemon Mold

2 cups cold water
1 6-oz. pkg. lemon flavored
    gelatin
1 6-oz. can frozen lemonade
    concentrate
½ cup MIRACLE WHIP Salad
    Dressing
1½ cups thawed frozen whipped
    topping
1 11-oz. can mandarin orange
    segments, drained
1 cup blueberries

Bring water to boil. Gradually add to gelatin, stirring until dissolved. Add concentrate; stir until melted. Cool. Gradually add to salad dressing, mixing until blended. Cover; chill until thickened but not set. Fold in whipped topping and fruit. Pour into 9-inch square pan; chill until firm. Cut into squares. Makes 8 to 10 servings.

Preparation time: 2 hours plus final chilling

Variation: Substitute 2-quart serving bowl for 9-inch square pan.

Walnut-Grape Salad

Cinnamon-Apple Coleslaw

- **3 cups shredded green cabbage**
- **2 cups shredded red cabbage**
- **1½ cups chopped apples**
- **1 cup MIRACLE WHIP Salad Dressing**
- **1 tablespoon honey**
- **½ teaspoon ground cinnamon**

Combine all ingredients; mix lightly. Cover; chill. Garnish with apple slices, if desired. Makes 6 servings.

Preparation time: 20 minutes plus chilling

Variations: Add ½ cup chopped walnuts, toasted, just before serving.

Honey-Mustard Coleslaw: Omit apples and cinnamon. Add 1 cup shredded carrot and 2 teaspoons KRAFT Pure Prepared Mustard.

Pineapple-Bacon Coleslaw: Omit apples, honey and cinnamon. Add 8-oz. can crushed pineapple, drained, 1 cup shredded carrot and 4 crisply cooked bacon slices, crumbled, just before serving.

Traditional Coleslaw: Omit 2 cups red cabbage; increase green cabbage to 5 cups. Omit apples and honey. Add 1 cup shredded carrot and ¾ teaspoon celery seed.

Substitute MIRACLE WHIP Light Reduced Calorie Salad Dressing with no cholesterol for Regular Salad Dressing.

Raspberry-Lemon Gelatin Salad

- **1 10-oz. pkg. frozen raspberries, thawed**
- **Cold water**
- **1 3-oz. pkg. raspberry flavored gelatin**
- **1 envelope unflavored gelatin**
- **½ cup lemon juice**
- **1 3½-oz. pkg. lemon instant pudding and pie filling mix**
- **2 cups cold milk**
- **1 cup MIRACLE WHIP Salad Dressing**

Drain raspberries, reserving liquid. Add enough water to reserved liquid to measure ¾ cup; set aside. Bring 1 cup water to boil. Gradually add to raspberry flavored gelatin, stirring until dissolved. Stir in reserved raspberry liquid. Cover; chill until thickened but not set. Fold in raspberries. Pour into 1½-quart clear serving bowl. Cover; chill until almost set. Combine unflavored gelatin and juice in small saucepan; let stand 1 minute. Stir over low heat until gelatin is dissolved. Cool. Combine pudding mix and milk; mix as directed on package for pudding. Stir in salad dressing. Gradually add gelatin mixture, mixing until well blended. Pour over raspberry layer; cover. Chill until firm. Makes 8 to 10 servings.

Preparation time: 1½ hours plus final chilling

Cinnamon-Apple Coleslaw

Cranberry Holiday Ring

2¼ cups cold water
1 3-oz. pkg. strawberry flavored gelatin
1 10½-oz. can frozen cranberry-orange relish, thawed
1 8-oz. can crushed pineapple
1 3-oz. pkg. lemon flavored gelatin
2 cups KRAFT Miniature Marshmallows
½ cup MIRACLE WHIP Salad Dressing
1 cup whipping cream, whipped

Bring 1 cup water to boil. Gradually add to strawberry gelatin, stirring until dissolved. Add cranberry-orange relish; mix well. Pour into lightly oiled 6½-cup ring mold; cover. Chill until almost set. Drain pineapple, reserving liquid. Bring remaining water to boil. Gradually add to lemon gelatin, stirring until dissolved. Add marshmallows; stir until melted. Add reserved pineapple liquid; cover. Chill until partially set. Add salad dressing and pineapple to marshmallow mixture. Fold in whipped cream; pour over strawberry layer. Cover; chill until firm. Unmold. Garnish as desired. Makes 12 servings.

Preparation time: 1½ hours plus final chilling

Variations: Substitute 12×8-inch baking dish for ring mold. Do not unmold.

Omit cranberry-orange relish. In 2-quart saucepan, combine 2 cups cranberries, ¾ cup sugar, ½ cup orange juice and 1 tablespoon grated orange peel; bring to boil. Reduce heat. Simmer 10 minutes over medium heat, stirring occasionally. Add to dissolved strawberry gelatin. Continue as directed.

Fruit Cloud

1 cup cold water
1 3-oz. pkg. orange flavored gelatin
½ cup MIRACLE WHIP Salad Dressing
2 cups thawed frozen whipped topping
1 17-oz. can fruit cocktail, drained
1 11-oz. can mandarin orange segments, drained
1 cup (4 ozs.) 100% Natural KRAFT Shredded Sharp Cheddar Cheese

Bring water to boil. Gradually add to gelatin, stirring until dissolved. Cool slightly. Gradually add gelatin to salad dressing, mixing until well blended. Cover; chill until thickened but not set, stirring occasionally. Fold in remaining ingredients. Cover; chill. Makes 4 to 6 servings.

Preparation time: 1 hour 15 minutes plus final chilling

Variations: Substitute 1 cup cottage cheese for shredded cheddar cheese.

Substitute 2½ to 3 cups chopped fresh fruit for canned fruit.

Cranberry Holiday Ring

Garden Salad

½ cup MIRACLE WHIP Salad
    Dressing
¼ teaspoon dill weed
2 cups cauliflowerets
1 cup cut green beans
1 cup green pepper chunks
    Salt and black pepper
1 cup cherry tomato halves

Combine salad dressing and dill weed; mix well. Add cauliflowerets, beans and pepper chunks; mix lightly. Season with salt and black pepper to taste. Cover; chill. Stir in tomatoes just before serving. Makes 6 to 8 servings.

Preparation time: 15 minutes plus chilling

Variation: Substitute MIRACLE WHIP Light Reduced Calorie Salad Dressing with no cholesterol for Regular Salad Dressing.

Heavenly Seven-Layer Salad

1½ quarts shredded lettuce
2 cups chopped tomatoes
2 cups mushroom slices
1 10-oz. pkg. frozen peas,
    thawed, drained
4 ozs. 100% Natural KRAFT Mild
    Cheddar Cheese, cubed
1 cup red onion rings
2 cups MIRACLE WHIP Light
    Reduced Calorie Salad
    Dressing with no cholesterol

In 2-quart serving bowl, layer lettuce, tomatoes, mushrooms, peas, cheese and onions. Spread salad dressing over onions, sealing to edge of bowl; cover. Chill several hours or overnight. Garnish with crisply cooked bacon slices, crumbled, and additional cheddar cheese, shredded, if desired. Makes 8 servings.

Preparation time: 15 minutes plus chilling

Kids' Favorite Fruit Salad

1 orange, peeled, cut into
    4 slices
    Leaf lettuce (optional)
2 medium bananas, cut into
    ½-inch slices
¼ cup MIRACLE WHIP Salad
    Dressing
½ cup finely chopped peanuts
4 maraschino cherries

For each salad, place one orange slice on lettuce-covered salad plate. Spread one side of each banana slice with salad dressing; dip into peanuts. Arrange bananas, peanut side up, around oranges. Place cherry in center. Makes 4 servings.

Preparation time: 10 minutes

Garden Salad

Potato & Pasta Salads

All-time favorites, potato and pasta salads, take on new twists and contemporary flavors. Try one of these irresistible salads at your next family gathering. Pictured here is Italian Pasta Salad; see page 42 for recipe.

Italian Pasta Salad

½ cup MIRACLE WHIP Salad
    Dressing
¼ cup (1 oz.) KRAFT 100%
    Grated Parmesan Cheese
¼ cup chopped parsley
2 tablespoons milk
3 ozs. spaghetti, broken into
    thirds, cooked, drained
1 cup salami or ham strips
1 cup carrot slices
1 cup zucchini slices
¼ cup pitted ripe olive slices

Combine salad dressing, cheese, parsley and milk; mix well. Add remaining ingredients; toss lightly. Cover; chill. Add additional salad dressing just before serving, if desired. Makes 4 to 6 servings.

Preparation time: 20 minutes plus chilling

One Pot Pasta Salad

2 cups (8 ozs.) corkscrew
    noodles
1 16-oz. pkg. frozen broccoli, red
    peppers, bamboo shoots and
    mushrooms
½ cup MIRACLE WHIP Salad
    Dressing
⅓ cup KRAFT "Zesty" Italian
    Dressing
¼ cup (1 oz.) KRAFT 100%
    Grated Parmesan Cheese

Cook noodles as directed on package, adding vegetables during last 2 minutes of cooking. Drain; rinse under cold running water until cooled. Combine remaining ingredients; mix well. Add noodles and vegetables; mix lightly. Serve at room temperature or chilled. Makes 4 to 6 servings.

Preparation time: 15 minutes

Variations: Substitute any 16-oz. pkg. frozen mixed vegetables for broccoli, red peppers, bamboo shoots and mushrooms.

Substitute MIRACLE WHIP Light Reduced Calorie Salad Dressing with no cholesterol for Regular Salad Dressing and KRAFT "Zesty" Reduced Calorie Italian Dressing for Regular Italian Dressing.

Southwestern-Style Potato Salad

¾ cup MIRACLE WHIP Salad
    Dressing
1 tablespoon chili sauce
1 garlic clove, minced
¼ teaspoon dried oregano leaves,
    crushed
¼ teaspoon ground cumin
4 cups cubed cooked potatoes
1 8½-oz. can whole kernel corn,
    drained
½ cup diagonally cut green onion
    slices
½ cup chopped red or green
    pepper
½ cup pitted ripe olive slices
2 tablespoons chopped cilantro

Combine salad dressing, chili sauce, garlic and seasonings; mix well. Add remaining ingredients; mix lightly. Serve at room temperature or chilled. Garnish as desired. Makes 6 to 8 servings.

Preparation time: 20 minutes

Variation: Substitute parsley for cilantro.

Southwestern-Style Potato Salad

Great American Potato Salad

1 cup MIRACLE WHIP Salad Dressing
1 teaspoon KRAFT Pure Prepared Mustard
1/2 teaspoon celery seed
1/2 teaspoon salt
1/8 teaspoon pepper
4 cups cubed cooked potatoes
2 hard-cooked eggs, chopped
1/2 cup chopped onion
1/2 cup celery slices
1/2 cup chopped sweet pickle

Combine salad dressing, mustard, celery seed, salt and pepper; mix well. Add remaining ingredients; mix lightly. Cover; chill. Makes 6 servings.

Preparation time: 30 minutes plus chilling

Variations: Omit celery and pickle. Add 1 1/2 cups chopped ham and 1/2 cup chopped green pepper.

Omit celery seed, celery and pickles. Add 1 cup chopped cucumber and 1/2 teaspoon dill weed.

Omit mustard, celery seed and pickles. Add 3 tablespoons SAUCEWORKS Horseradish Sauce and 1 1/2 cups cubed roast beef.

Pesto Pasta Salad

1/2 cup MIRACLE WHIP Salad Dressing
1/2 cup fresh prepared pesto
6 ozs. mostaccioli noodles, cooked, drained
2 cups mushroom halves
1 cup red pepper strips

Combine salad dressing and pesto; mix well. Add remaining ingredients; mix lightly. Cover; chill. Makes 4 to 6 servings.

Preparation time: 20 minutes plus chilling

Summer Pasta Salad

1/2 cup MIRACLE WHIP Light Reduced Calorie Salad Dressing with no cholesterol
1/4 cup (1 oz.) KRAFT 100% Grated Parmesan Cheese
2 tablespoons milk
1 1/2 cups chopped cooked chicken
1 cup (4 ozs.) shell macaroni, cooked, drained
1 cup cherry tomato halves
1 cup green pepper chunks
2 tablespoons chopped onion
1/2 teaspoon salt

Combine salad dressing, cheese and milk; mix well. Add remaining ingredients; mix lightly. Cover; chill. Add additional salad dressing just before serving, if desired. Makes 4 servings.

Preparation time: 15 minutes plus chilling

Variations: Add 1/4 teaspoon dried basil leaves, crushed, to salad dressing mixture.

Omit salt. Substitute ham for chicken.

Great American Potato Salad

Seafood Pasta Salad

- ½ cup MIRACLE WHIP Salad Dressing
- ¼ cup KRAFT "Zesty" Italian Dressing
- 2 tablespoons KRAFT 100% Grated Parmesan Cheese
- 2 cups (8 ozs.) corkscrew noodles, cooked, drained
- 1½ cups (8 ozs.) chopped imitation crabmeat
- 1 cup broccoli flowerets, partially cooked
- ½ cup chopped green pepper
- ½ cup chopped tomato
- ¼ cup green onion slices

Combine dressings and cheese; mix well. Add remaining ingredients; mix lightly. Cover; chill. Serve with freshly ground black pepper, if desired. Makes 4 servings.

Preparation time: 15 minutes plus chilling

Variation: Substitute MIRACLE WHIP Light Reduced Calorie Salad Dressing with no cholesterol for Regular Salad Dressing and KRAFT "Zesty" Reduced Calorie Italian Dressing for Regular Italian Dressing.

Cucumber-Dill Potato Salad

- ⅔ cup MIRACLE WHIP Light Reduced Calorie Salad Dressing with no cholesterol
- ¼ teaspoon salt
- ¼ teaspoon dill weed
- 4 cups cubed cooked potatoes
- 1 cup chopped cucumber
- ¾ cup carrot slices
- 1 tablespoon chopped chives

Combine salad dressing and seasonings; mix well. Add remaining ingredients; mix lightly. Cover; chill. Add additional salad dressing just before serving, if desired. Makes 4 to 6 servings.

Preparation time: 30 minutes plus chilling

Microwave Potato Salad

- 4 cups cubed potatoes
- ⅓ cup cold water
- 1 cup MIRACLE WHIP Salad Dressing
- ⅓ cup KRAFT "Zesty" Italian Dressing
- ¼ cup (1 oz.) KRAFT 100% Grated Parmesan Cheese
- 1 16-oz. pkg. frozen broccoli, green beans, pearl onions and red peppers, thawed
  Salt and pepper

MICROWAVE: Combine potatoes and water in 2-quart microwave-safe casserole; cover. Microwave on High 8 to 12 minutes or until tender, stirring after 6 minutes. Drain. Combine dressings; mix well. Add potatoes, cheese and vegetables; mix lightly. Season with salt and pepper to taste. Cover; chill. Makes 4 to 6 servings.

Preparation time: 20 minutes plus chilling

Variations: Substitute any 16-oz. pkg. frozen mixed vegetables for frozen broccoli, green beans, pearl onions and red peppers.

Substitute MIRACLE WHIP Light Reduced Calorie Salad Dressing with no cholesterol for Regular Salad Dressing.

Seafood Pasta Salad

Main-Dish Salads

These memorable main-dish salads tempt your taste buds with their range of savory flavors. The salads in this chapter make a perfect lunch or light dinner meal. Pictured here is Chicken Chutney Salad; see page 50 for recipe.

Chicken Chutney Salad

¾ cup MIRACLE WHIP Salad Dressing
¼ cup mango chutney
4 cups cubed cooked chicken
1 cup chopped jicama
1 cup red grape halves
½ cup chopped celery
  Salt and pepper
½ cup coarsely chopped pecans, toasted
4 crisply cooked bacon slices, crumbled (optional)

Combine salad dressing and chutney; mix well. Add chicken, jicama, grapes and celery; mix lightly. Season with salt and pepper to taste. Cover; chill. Add pecans and bacon just before serving; mix lightly. Serve with croissants, if desired. Makes 6 servings.

Preparation time: 15 minutes plus chilling

Pizza Lovers' Salad

½ cup MIRACLE WHIP Salad Dressing
½ teaspoon Italian seasoning
1 qt. torn romaine lettuce
1 tomato, chopped
½ cup chopped red or green pepper
½ cup sliced mushrooms
½ cup red onion rings
2 ozs. CASINO Brand Natural Low Moisture Part-Skim Mozzarella Cheese, cubed
½ cup julienne-cut salami
½ cup seasoned croutons

Combine salad dressing and seasoning in large bowl; mix well. Add remaining ingredients except croutons; mix lightly. Serve on salad plates; top with croutons. Garnish as desired. Makes 6 servings.

Preparation time: 20 minutes

Northwest Macaroni Salad

½ cup MIRACLE WHIP Salad Dressing
2 teaspoons KRAFT Pure Prepared Mustard
¾ lb. smoked sausage, cut into ¼-inch slices, halved
1 cup (3½ ozs.) elbow macaroni, cooked, drained
1 8-oz. can pineapple tidbits, drained
⅓ cup chopped green pepper
2 tablespoons chopped onion
  Salt and pepper

Combine salad dressing and mustard, mixing until well blended. Add sausage, macaroni, pineapple, peppers and onions; mix lightly. Season with salt and pepper to taste. Cover; chill. Add additional salad dressing just before serving, if desired. Makes 4 to 6 servings.

Preparation time: 15 minutes plus chilling

Pizza Lovers' Salad

Cajun Chicken Salad

3/4 cup MIRACLE WHIP Salad
    Dressing
1 teaspoon ground cumin
1/2 teaspoon ground red pepper
1/8 teaspoon salt
4 cups chopped cooked chicken
1/2 cup chopped celery
1/4 cup chopped red or green
    pepper
2 tablespoons finely chopped
    onion
1 garlic clove, minced

Combine salad dressing and seasonings; mix well. Add remaining ingredients; mix lightly. Cover; chill. Add additional salad dressing just before serving, if desired. Makes 4 to 6 servings.

Preparation time: 15 minutes plus chilling

Variation: Substitute MIRACLE WHIP Light Reduced Calorie Salad Dressing with no cholesterol for Regular Salad Dressing.

Nautical Salad

3/4 cup MIRACLE WHIP Salad
    Dressing
1/2 cup sour cream
1/4 cup chopped cucumber
2 tablespoons finely chopped
    onion
2 hard-cooked eggs
1/2 teaspoon dill weed
    Lettuce
2 6 1/2-oz. cans tuna, drained,
    flaked

Combine salad dressing, sour cream, cucumbers, onions, chopped egg whites and dill weed; mix well. Cover; chill. To serve, cover lettuce-lined salad plate with tuna. Top with salad dressing mixture and sieved egg yolks. Garnish as desired. Makes 4 servings.

Preparation time: 25 minutes plus chilling

Variations: Substitute MIRACLE WHIP Light Reduced Calorie Salad Dressing with no cholesterol for Regular Salad Dressing and plain yogurt for sour cream.

Substitute one 15 1/2-oz. can salmon for two 6 1/2-oz. cans tuna.

Recipe tip: To sieve egg yolk, place yolk in small wire strainer. Using back of spoon, gently push yolk through strainer.

Ham & Pasta Salad

2 cups (7 ozs.) medium shell
    macaroni, cooked, drained
1 cup frozen peas, thawed,
    drained
1 cup ham cubes
1/2 cup MIRACLE WHIP Salad
    Dressing
1 hard-cooked egg, chopped
2 tablespoons chopped onion
    Salt and pepper

Combine ingredients except salt and pepper; mix lightly. Season with salt and pepper to taste. Cover; chill. Add additional salad dressing just before serving, if desired. Makes 4 to 6 servings.

Preparation time: 25 minutes plus chilling

Nautical Salad

Jambalaya Salad

½ cup MIRACLE WHIP Salad
   Dressing
½ teaspoon dried thyme leaves,
   crushed
⅛ teaspoon ground red pepper
1 garlic clove, minced
2 cups cooked rice
1 cup chopped tomato
1 6-oz. pkg. frozen cooked tiny
   shrimp, thawed
½ cup ham cubes
½ cup chopped green pepper
¼ cup chopped onion
6 crisply cooked bacon slices,
   crumbled

Combine salad dressing, seasonings and garlic; mix well. Add remaining ingredients except bacon; mix lightly. Cover; chill. Add bacon just before serving; mix lightly. Garnish as desired. Makes 4 to 6 servings.

Preparation time: 25 minutes plus chilling

Layered Taco Salad

4 chicken breast halves, boned,
   skinned, cubed
1 tablespoon oil
¾ cup salsa
   Guacamole (recipe follows)
3 cups coarsely broken tortilla
   chips
1 qt. torn lettuce
1 15-oz. can kidney beans,
   drained, rinsed
1 cup (4 ozs.) 100% Natural
   KRAFT Shredded Sharp
   Cheddar Cheese
2 crisply cooked bacon slices,
   crumbled

Stir-fry chicken in oil in 10-inch skillet over medium-high heat 4 to 5 minutes or until tender. Reduce heat to medium. Stir in salsa; cover. Simmer 5 minutes. Prepare Guacamole. In 3- to 4-quart serving bowl, layer chips, lettuce, beans and chicken mixture. Cover with Guacamole, spreading to edges of bowl to seal. Sprinkle with cheese. Cover; chill. Add bacon; toss lightly just before serving. Makes 8 servings.

Guacamole

1 ripe avocado, peeled, mashed
½ cup MIRACLE WHIP Salad
   Dressing
½ cup salsa

Combine ingredients; mix well. Makes approximately 1¼ cups.

Preparation time: 20 minutes plus chilling

Microwave tip: Omit oil. To cook chicken, place chicken in 1½-quart microwave-safe casserole; cover. Microwave on High 4 to 5 minutes or until tender, stirring every 2 minutes. Drain; stir in salsa. Microwave on High 1 minute.

Jambalaya Salad

Entrees

Variety is highlighted in these appealing main-dish recipes— casseroles, stir-fries, sandwiches, and more, using seafood, poultry, meats and dairy products. There's something for everyone's taste. Pictured here is Crab & Broccoli Frittata; see page 58 for recipe.

Crab & Broccoli Frittata

6 eggs, beaten
1/3 cup MIRACLE WHIP Salad Dressing
1 1/2 cups 100% Natural KRAFT Shredded Sharp Cheddar Cheese
1 cup chopped broccoli, cooked, drained
1 1/2 cups chopped imitation crabmeat
Dash of pepper

Combine eggs and salad dressing; mix well. Stir in 1 cup cheese, broccoli, crabmeat and pepper. Pour into well-greased 9-inch pie plate or 10-inch ovenproof skillet. Bake at 350°, 25 minutes or until set. Top with remaining cheese; continue baking 5 minutes or until cheese is melted. Cut into wedges to serve. Makes 6 servings.

Preparation time: 10 minutes

Baking time: 30 minutes

MICROWAVE: In medium microwave-safe bowl, combine eggs, salad dressing, 1 cup cheese, broccoli, crabmeat and pepper. Microwave on High 2 minutes, stirring after each minute. Pour into 9-inch microwave-safe pie plate or 10×6-inch microwave-safe baking dish. Cover with plastic wrap; vent. Microwave on High 7 to 9 minutes or until almost set, turning dish every 4 minutes. Top with remaining cheese. Let stand, covered, 5 minutes. Cut into wedges to serve.

Fettucini Italiano

8 ozs. fettucini
1/3 cup MIRACLE WHIP Light Reduced Calorie Salad Dressing with no cholesterol
1 garlic clove, minced
1/2 cup milk
5 crisply cooked bacon slices, crumbled
1/3 cup (1 1/2 ozs.) KRAFT 100% Grated Parmesan Cheese
1/4 cup chopped parsley

Prepare fettucini as directed on package; drain. Combine salad dressing and garlic in small saucepan. Gradually stir in milk; heat thoroughly, stirring occasionally. Toss with hot fettucini until well coated. Add remaining ingredients; toss lightly. Makes 5 servings.

Preparation time: 25 minutes

Variations: Substitute spaghetti for fettucini.

Substitute MIRACLE WHIP Salad Dressing for Reduced Calorie Salad Dressing with no cholesterol.

MICROWAVE: Prepare fettucini as directed on package; drain. Combine salad dressing and garlic in 2-quart microwave-safe bowl; gradually add milk. Microwave on High 1 1/2 to 2 minutes or until thoroughly heated, stirring after 1 minute. (Do not boil.) Add hot fettucini; toss until well coated. Continue as directed.

Fettucini Italiano

Baked Chicken Parmesan

1 cup cornflake crumbs
½ cup (2 ozs.) KRAFT 100%
  Grated Parmesan Cheese
Dash of salt and pepper
1 2½- to 3-lb. broiler-fryer, cut
  up, skinned
¾ cup MIRACLE WHIP Salad
  Dressing

Combine crumbs, cheese, salt and pepper. Brush chicken with salad dressing; coat with crumb mixture. Place in 13×9-inch baking dish. Bake at 350°, 1 hour or until tender. Serve with your favorite accompaniments. Makes 3 to 4 servings.

Preparation time: 15 minutes

Baking time: 1 hour

Variations: For Cajun Chicken, omit salt. Add 1 teaspoon *each* ground cumin and onion powder and ½ teaspoon *each* ground red pepper and garlic powder to salad dressing; mix well. Substitute 1½ cups crushed sesame crackers for cornflake crumbs and parmesan cheese. Continue as directed.

Substitute MIRACLE WHIP Light Reduced Calorie Salad Dressing with no cholesterol for Regular Salad Dressing.

MICROWAVE: Substitute 12×8-inch microwave-safe baking dish for 13×9-inch baking dish. Coat chicken as directed. Arrange in baking dish with meatiest portions toward outside of dish. Microwave on High 17 to 20 minutes or until chicken is tender, turning dish after 8 minutes. Let stand 5 minutes. Serve with your favorite accompaniment.

Swiss Club Bundles

¾ cup (3 ozs.) 100% Natural
  KRAFT Shredded Swiss
  Cheese
1 cup finely chopped ham
½ cup MIRACLE WHIP Salad
  Dressing
¼ cup green onion slices
2 tablespoons KRAFT 100%
  Grated Parmesan Cheese
4 6-inch French bread rolls,
  partially split

Combine ingredients except rolls; mix lightly. Fill rolls with ham mixture; wrap in foil. Bake at 350°, 15 minutes or until thoroughly heated. Makes 8 sandwiches.

Preparation time: 10 minutes

Baking time 15 minutes

Variations: Substitute hamburger buns for French bread rolls.

Substitute cooked turkey or chicken for ham.

Baked Chicken Parmesan

Oriental Pork

½ cup MIRACLE WHIP Salad
   Dressing
3 tablespoons peanut butter
1 tablespoon soy sauce
½ teaspoon ground ginger
2 tablespoons oil
2 cups diagonally cut celery
   slices
1 red or green pepper, cut into
   chunks
¼ cup green onion slices
1 garlic clove, minced
1 lb. lean pork, cut into ½-inch
   strips
3 cups shredded lettuce

Combine salad dressing, peanut butter, soy sauce and ginger; mix well. Set aside. Heat 1 tablespoon oil in large skillet or wok over medium-high heat 1 minute. Add vegetables and garlic; stir-fry 4 minutes or until crisp-tender. Remove vegetables and garlic from skillet; add remaining oil to skillet. Add pork; stir-fry 9 to 10 minutes or until pork is no longer pink. Return vegetables to skillet. Add salad dressing mixture; mix lightly. Serve over lettuce. Makes 4 servings.

Preparation time: 30 minutes

Cooking time: 20 minutes

MICROWAVE: Omit oil. Combine salad dressing, peanut butter, soy sauce and ginger; mix well. Set aside. Place vegetables and garlic in medium microwave-safe bowl. Cover with plastic wrap; vent. Microwave on High 3½ to 4 minutes or until vegetables are crisp-tender, stirring after 2 minutes. Set aside. Place meat in 2-quart microwave-safe casserole; cover. Microwave on High 5 to 6 minutes or until pork is no longer pink, stirring every 2 minutes; drain. Add salad dressing mixture and reserved vegetables; mix well. Microwave, covered, on High 1 to 2 minutes or until thoroughly heated. Serve as directed.

Zucchini Ham Bake

4 cups thinly sliced zucchini
1 cup sliced mushrooms
½ cup onion rings
1 garlic clove, minced
1 teaspoon Italian seasoning
1 egg, beaten
⅔ cup MIRACLE WHIP Salad
   Dressing
½ cup sour cream
1 tablespoon flour
2 cups chopped ham
1 cup (4 ozs.) shredded CASINO
   Brand Natural Monterey Jack
   Cheese

Combine zucchini, mushrooms, onions, garlic and seasoning; mix lightly. Combine egg, salad dressing, sour cream and flour, mixing until well blended. In greased 12×8-inch baking dish, layer half the vegetable mixture, salad dressing mixture, ham and cheese; repeat layers. Bake at 350°, 30 minutes or until thoroughly heated. Makes 6 servings.

Preparation time: 20 minutes

Baking time: 30 minutes

Eggplant Rolls

1 10-oz. pkg. frozen chopped
    spinach, thawed, well
    drained
1 cup ricotta cheese
2/3 cup MIRACLE WHIP Salad
    Dressing
1 large eggplant, peeled, cut
    lengthwise into 8 slices
1/2 cup dry bread crumbs
2 to 3 tablespoons oil
1 15½-oz. jar spaghetti sauce
1/2 cup (2 ozs.) 100% Natural
    KRAFT Shredded Low
    Moisture Part-Skim
    Mozzarella Cheese
1/4 cup (1 oz.) KRAFT 100%
    Grated Parmesan Cheese

Combine spinach, ricotta cheese and 1/3 cup salad dressing; mix lightly. Brush both sides of eggplant slices generously with remaining salad dressing; coat with crumbs. Heat 2 tablespoons oil in large skillet over medium-high heat. Add eggplant, two slices at a time. Cook over medium heat until tender and lightly browned, adding additional oil as necessary. Spread approximately 1/4 cup spinach mixture onto each eggplant slice. Roll up, starting at narrow end. Place, seam-side down, in 8-inch square baking dish. Top with spaghetti sauce and cheeses. Bake at 350°, 30 minutes or until thoroughly heated. Makes 4 servings.

Preparation time: 40 minutes

Baking time: 30 minutes

MICROWAVE: Assemble recipe as directed except for topping with cheeses. Place, seam-side down, in 8-inch square microwave-safe baking dish. Cover with wax paper. Microwave on High 11 to 12 minutes or until thoroughly heated, turning dish every 4 minutes. Top with cheeses. Microwave, uncovered, on High 1½ to 2 minutes or until mozzarella cheese is melted.

Microwave tip: To thaw spinach, place frozen spinach in 1-quart microwave-safe casserole; cover. Microwave on High 3½ minutes. Break apart with fork; drain well.

Beach Picnic Sandwiches

2 cups shredded cabbage
    MIRACLE WHIP Salad Dressing
1/4 cup chopped green pepper
1/2 teaspoon celery seed
6 hard rolls, split
    Assorted luncheon meat slices
    100% Natural KRAFT Swiss or
      Muenster Cheese Slices, cut
      in half
    Tomato slices

Combine cabbage, 1/4 cup salad dressing, peppers and celery seed; mix lightly. Spread rolls with additional salad dressing; fill with cabbage mixture, meat, cheese and tomatoes. Makes 6 sandwiches.

Preparation time: 20 minutes

Variations: Substitute 100% Natural KRAFT Monterey Jack or Cheddar Cheese Slices for Swiss or Muenster Slices.

Substitute lettuce for cabbage, 3 whole-wheat pita bread rounds, cut in half, for 6 hard rolls, split, and turkey slices for assorted luncheon meat slices.

Substitute MIRACLE WHIP Light Reduced Calorie Salad Dressing with no cholesterol for Regular Salad Dressing.

Tasty Turkey Pot Pie

½ cup MIRACLE WHIP Salad
   Dressing
2 tablespoons flour
1 teaspoon instant chicken
   bouillon
⅛ teaspoon pepper
¾ cup milk
1½ cups chopped cooked turkey
   or chicken
1 10-oz. pkg. frozen mixed
   vegetables, thawed, drained
1 4-oz. can PILLSBURY
   Refrigerated Quick Crescent
   Dinner Rolls

Combine salad dressing, flour, bouillon and pepper in medium saucepan. Gradually add milk. Cook, stirring constantly, over low heat until thickened. Add turkey and vegetables; heat thoroughly, stirring occasionally. Spoon into 8-inch square baking dish. Unroll dough into two rectangles. Press perforations together to seal. Place rectangles side-by-side to form square; press edges together to form seam. Cover turkey mixture with dough. Bake at 375°, 15 to 20 minutes or until browned. Makes 4 to 6 servings.

Preparation time: 15 minutes

Baking time: 20 minutes

Variations: Combine 1 egg, beaten, and 1 tablespoon cold water, mixing until well blended. Brush dough with egg mixture just before baking.

Substitute one chicken bouillon cube for instant chicken bouillon.

Substitute 10×6-inch baking dish for 8-inch square baking dish.

Substitute 12×8-inch baking dish for 8-inch square dish. Double all ingredients. Assemble recipe as directed, using three dough rectangles to form top crust. Decorate crust with cut-outs from remaining rectangle. Bake as directed.

Microwave tip: To prepare sauce, combine salad dressing, flour, bouillon and pepper in 1-quart microwave-safe measure or bowl; gradually add milk. Microwave on High 4 to 5 minutes or until thickened, stirring after each minute.

"Just for Kids" Sandwich

¼ cup MIRACLE WHIP Salad
   Dressing
¼ cup peanut butter
½ cup chopped apple
¼ cup raisins
8 bread slices

Combine salad dressing and peanut butter, mixing until well blended. Stir in apples and raisins. For each sandwich, spread one bread slice with salad dressing mixture; top with second bread slice. Makes 4 sandwiches.

Preparation time: 10 minutes

Tasty Turkey Pot Pie

Almond-Chicken Casserole

    1 cup fresh bread cubes
    1 tablespoon PARKAY Margarine,
        melted
    3 cups chopped cooked chicken
1½ cups diagonally cut celery
        slices
    1 cup MIRACLE WHIP Salad
        Dressing
    1 cup (4 ozs.) shredded 100%
        Natural KRAFT Swiss
        Cheese
    ½ cup 1½-inch-long red or green
        pepper strips
    ¼ cup slivered almonds, toasted
    ¼ cup chopped onion

Combine bread cubes and margarine; toss lightly. Set aside. Combine remaining ingredients; mix lightly. Spoon into 10×6-inch baking dish. Top with bread cubes. Bake at 350°, 30 minutes or until lightly browned. Garnish as desired. Makes 6 servings.

Preparation time: 20 minutes

Baking time: 30 minutes

MICROWAVE: Combine bread cubes and margarine in 9-inch microwave-safe pie plate; toss lightly. Microwave on High 2 minutes, stirring after 1 minute; set aside. Combine remaining ingredients in 10×6-inch microwave-safe baking dish. Microwave 3 minutes; stir. Top with bread cubes. Microwave 2 to 3 minutes or until thoroughly heated. Garnish as desired.

Almond-Chicken Casserole

Midwestern Stir-Fry

    ½ cup MIRACLE WHIP Salad
        Dressing
    2 tablespoons milk
    ½ teaspoon KRAFT Pure
        Prepared Mustard
    ½ lb. smoked sausage, cut into
        ¼-inch slices, halved
    ¾ cup yellow squash slices,
        halved
    ½ cup green or red pepper strips
    ½ cup 1-inch green onion pieces
        Hot cooked rice

Combine salad dressing, milk and mustard, mixing until well blended; set aside. Stir-fry sausage in large skillet or wok over high heat until thoroughly heated. Remove sausage from skillet; drain, reserving 1 tablespoon fat. Return reserved fat to skillet. Add squash and peppers. Stir-fry 3 minutes. Return sausage to skillet with onions; stir-fry 1 minute. Remove from heat. Add salad dressing mixture; mix lightly. Serve over hot cooked rice. Makes 4 servings.

Preparation time: 10 minutes

Cooking time: 10 minutes

MICROWAVE: Combine salad dressing, milk and mustard, mixing until well blended; set aside. Combine sausage, peppers and onions in medium microwave-safe bowl. Microwave on High 2 minutes. Stir in squash. Continue microwaving on High 2 minutes or until vegetables are crisp-tender. Add salad dressing mixture; mix lightly. Microwave on Medium (50%) 2 to 3 minutes or until thoroughly heated, stirring after 2 minutes. Do not overheat. Serve over hot cooked rice.

Parmesan Turkey Divan

¼ cup PARKAY Margarine
¼ cup flour
1½ cups milk
⅓ cup MIRACLE WHIP Salad Dressing
2 10-oz. pkgs. frozen broccoli spears, thawed, drained
½ cup (2 ozs.) KRAFT 100% Grated Parmesan Cheese
6 cooked turkey slices, ¼ inch thick (approx. ¾ lb.)

Melt margarine in saucepan over low heat. Blend in flour. Gradually add milk; cook, stirring constantly, until thickened. Stir in salad dressing. Arrange broccoli in 12×8-inch baking dish; sprinkle with ¼ cup cheese. Top with turkey, salad dressing mixture and remaining cheese. Bake at 350°, 35 to 40 minutes or until thoroughly heated. Makes 6 to 8 servings.

Preparation time: 20 minutes

Baking time: 40 minutes

Make ahead: Prepare recipe as directed except for baking. Cover with foil; chill. When ready to serve, bake, covered, at 350°, 30 minutes. Remove cover; continue baking 20 minutes or until thoroughly heated.

MICROWAVE: Microwave margarine in 1-quart microwave-safe measure on High 1 minute or until melted. Blend in flour; microwave on High 1 minute. Gradually add milk; microwave on High 4 to 5 minutes or until thickened, stirring well after each minute. Stir in salad dressing. Using 12×8-inch microwave-safe casserole, assemble recipe as directed. Cover with plastic wrap; vent. Microwave on High 8 to 9 minutes or until thoroughly heated, turning dish every 3 minutes.

Easy Ham & Potatoes au Gratin

1 lb. (3½ cups) frozen hash brown potatoes, thawed
1½ cups chopped ham
1 cup (4 ozs.) 100% Natural KRAFT Shredded Sharp Cheddar Cheese
½ cup MIRACLE WHIP Salad Dressing
½ cup milk
½ cup fresh bread crumbs
1 tablespoon PARKAY Margarine, melted
Salt and pepper

Combine potatoes, ham and cheese; mix lightly. Combine salad dressing and milk; mix well. Add salad dressing mixture to potato mixture; mix lightly. Spoon into 1-quart casserole. Combine crumbs and margarine; sprinkle over potato mixture. Bake at 350°, 40 to 45 minutes or until thoroughly heated. Season with salt and pepper to taste. Makes 4 to 6 servings.

Preparation time: 10 minutes

Baking time: 45 minutes

Variation: Omit ham. Add ¼ cup chopped onion.

Make ahead: Prepare recipe as directed except for baking. Cover; chill. When ready to serve, remove cover. Bake at 350°, 1 hour or until thoroughly heated.

MICROWAVE: Reduce milk to ⅓ cup. Substitute 1½-quart microwave-safe casserole for 1-quart casserole. Microwave margarine in 1½-quart microwave-safe casserole on High 30 seconds or until melted; stir in crumbs. Microwave on High 2 minutes. Remove from casserole; set aside. Combine remaining ingredients as directed in 1½-quart microwave-safe casserole; cover. Microwave on High 10 to 12 minutes or until thoroughly heated, stirring every 4 minutes. Stir; sprinkle with reserved crumbs. Let stand 5 minutes.

Microwave tip: To thaw potatoes, place potatoes in 1½-quart microwave-safe casserole. Microwave on Medium (50%) 5 to 6 minutes or until thawed, stirring after 3 minutes.

Chicken Dijon

½ cup MIRACLE WHIP Salad
    Dressing
¼ cup dijon mustard
1 2½- to 3-lb. broiler-fryer, cut
    up, skinned
1¼ cups dry bread crumbs
¼ cup PARKAY Margarine, melted

Combine salad dressing and mustard, mixing until well blended. Brush chicken with salad dressing mixture; coat with crumbs. Place in 13×9-inch baking dish; drizzle with margarine. Bake at 350°, 1 hour or until chicken is tender. Makes 4 servings.

Preparation time: 25 minutes

Baking time: 1 hour

Variation: Substitute MIRACLE WHIP Light Reduced Calorie Salad Dressing with no cholesterol for Regular Salad Dressing.

MICROWAVE: Substitute 12×8-inch microwave-safe baking dish for 13×9-inch baking dish. Add ½ teaspoon paprika to crumbs. Coat chicken as directed. Arrange in baking dish with meatiest portions toward outside of dish; drizzle with margarine. Microwave on High 17 to 20 minutes or until chicken is tender, turning dish after 8 minutes. Let stand 5 minutes.

Country Chicken Bake

1 cup uncooked rice
1 cup celery slices
3/4 cup chopped onion
2 teaspoons parsley flakes
1/8 teaspoon pepper
1 10 3/4-oz. can condensed cream of mushroom soup
3/4 cup MIRACLE WHIP Salad Dressing
1 3/4 cups cold water
6 chicken breast halves, skinned

Place rice in greased 12×8-inch baking dish. Combine vegetables and seasonings; spoon over rice. Combine soup and salad dressing; mix well. Gradually add water to soup mixture, mixing until well blended. Pour half the soup mixture over vegetables; top with chicken and remaining soup mixture. Bake at 350°, 1 hour or until chicken is tender and rice is cooked. Sprinkle with paprika, if desired. Makes 6 servings.

Preparation time: 15 minutes

Baking time: 1 hour

Variations: Substitute MIRACLE WHIP Light Reduced Calorie Salad Dressing with no cholesterol for Regular Salad Dressing.

Substitute boneless chicken breasts for chicken breasts. Reduce baking time to 45 minutes or until chicken is tender.

Pork Piccata

3/4 lb. pork tenderloin
1/2 cup MIRACLE WHIP Salad Dressing
1/4 cup seasoned bread crumbs
1 tablespoon KRAFT 100% Grated Parmesan Cheese
1 tablespoon PARKAY Margarine
1 garlic clove, minced
1 tablespoon milk
1 tablespoon capers, drained
1 teaspoon lemon juice

Slice pork into 3/4-inch slices; pound to 1/4-inch thickness. Spread pork generously with 1/4 cup salad dressing. Combine crumbs and cheese. Coat pork with crumb mixture. Melt margarine. Add garlic; cook until tender. Reduce heat. Add pork; cook over medium heat until meat is no longer pink. Combine remaining salad dressing, milk, capers and juice; mix well. Serve with pork. Serve with your favorite accompaniments. Makes 4 servings.

Preparation time: 20 minutes

Cooking time: 20 minutes

Pork Piccata

Stuffed Pasta Shells

    2 cups finely chopped cooked
        ham or turkey
    1 cup ricotta cheese
    ½ cup MIRACLE WHIP Salad
        Dressing
    ¼ cup chopped red onion
    4 ozs. (18) large pasta shells,
        cooked, drained
    2 tablespoons cold water
    ¼ cup (1 oz.) KRAFT 100%
        Grated Parmesan Cheese
    ¼ cup dry bread crumbs
    1 to 2 tablespoons chopped
        parsley
    1 tablespoon PARKAY Margarine

Combine ham, ricotta cheese, salad
dressing and onions; mix lightly.
Fill shells with ham mixture;
place, filled side up, in shallow
baking dish. Add 2 tablespoons
cold water to dish; cover with foil.
Bake at 350°, 30 minutes or until
thoroughly heated. Combine
parmesan cheese, crumbs, parsley
and margarine, melted; sprinkle
over shells. Continue baking,
uncovered, 5 minutes. Serve with
your favorite accompaniments.
Makes 6 servings.

Preparation time: 15 minutes

Baking time: 35 minutes

MICROWAVE: Omit cold water.
Microwave margarine in 9-inch
microwave-safe pie plate on High
30 seconds or until melted. Stir in
parmesan cheese and crumbs.
Microwave on High 2 minutes,
stirring after 1 minute. Stir in
parsley; set aside. Assemble shells
as directed; place in shallow
microwave-safe baking dish. Cover
with plastic wrap; vent. Microwave
on High 7 to 8 minutes or until
thoroughly heated, turning dish
after 4 minutes. Sprinkle with
parmesan cheese mixture. Let
stand 5 minutes. Serve with your
favorite accompaniments.

Gyros Sandwiches

    ½ lb. gyros meat
    4 pita bread rounds
        MIRACLE WHIP Salad Dressing
    4 ozs. feta cheese, crumbled
    ½ cup chopped cucumber
    ½ cup thin onion slices,
        separated into rings
        Chopped tomatoes

Brown meat. Lightly brush both
sides of bread rounds with salad
dressing. Place on cookie sheet;
sprinkle with cheese. Bake at 350°,
5 minutes. Combine cucumber,
onions and ⅓ cup salad dressing.
Cover bread rounds with meat,
salad dressing mixture and
tomatoes. Fold in half to serve.
Makes 4 sandwiches.

Preparation time: 20 minutes

Stuffed Pasta Shells

Cajun Baked Fish

1/3 cup MIRACLE WHIP Salad
    Dressing
1/2 teaspoon ground cumin
1/2 teaspoon onion powder
1/4 teaspoon ground red pepper
1/4 teaspoon garlic powder
  1 lb. fish fillets
1/2 cup crushed sesame crackers

Combine salad dressing and
seasonings; mix well. Brush fish
with salad dressing mixture; coat
with crumbs. Place in greased
shallow baking dish. Bake at 350°,
30 minutes or until fish begins to
flake when tested with a fork.
Serve with your favorite
accompaniments. Makes 3 to 4
servings.

Preparation time: 15 minutes

Baking time: 30 minutes

MICROWAVE: Combine salad
dressing and seasonings; mix well.
Brush fish with salad dressing
mixture; coat with crumbs.
Arrange fish in shallow microwave-
safe baking dish, placing thickest
portions toward outside of dish.
Cover with plastic wrap; vent.
Microwave on High 5 minutes,
turning dish after 3 minutes. Let
stand, covered, 2 to 3 minutes or
until fish begins to flake when
tested with a fork. Serve with your
favorite accompaniments.

Tuna-Broccoli Casserole

1 10 3/4-oz. can condensed cream
    of celery soup
1/2 cup MIRACLE WHIP Salad
    Dressing
1 cup (3 1/2 ozs.) elbow macaroni,
    cooked, drained
1 cup frozen cut broccoli,
    thawed
1 6 1/2-oz. can tuna, drained,
    flaked
1/2 cup chopped red or green
    pepper
1/4 cup chopped onion
1 cup shoestring potatoes

Combine soup and salad dressing;
mix well. Add all remaining
ingredients except potatoes; mix
lightly. Spoon into 1-quart
casserole; sprinkle with potatoes.
Bake at 350°, 30 minutes or until
thoroughly heated. Makes 6
servings.

Preparation time: 15 minutes

Baking time: 30 minutes

MICROWAVE: Using 1-quart
microwave-safe casserole, assemble
recipe as directed except for
topping with potatoes; cover.
Microwave on High 6 to 7 minutes
or until thoroughly heated, stirring
after 4 minutes. Stir; sprinkle with
potatoes. Let stand 5 minutes.

Microwave tip: To thaw broccoli,
place frozen broccoli in small
microwave-safe bowl. Cover with
plastic wrap; vent. Microwave on
High 1 to 1 1/2 minutes or until
thawed.

Cajun Baked Fish

Turkey Tetrazzini

⅔ cup MIRACLE WHIP Salad
    Dressing
⅓ cup flour
½ teaspoon celery salt
    Dash of pepper
2 cups milk
7 ozs. spaghetti, broken into
    thirds, cooked, drained
2 cups chopped cooked turkey
    or chicken
¾ cup (3 ozs.) KRAFT 100%
    Grated Parmesan Cheese
1 4-oz. can mushrooms, drained
2 tablespoons chopped pimento
    (optional)
2 cups fresh bread cubes
3 tablespoons PARKAY
    Margarine, melted

Combine salad dressing, flour and
seasonings in medium saucepan.
Gradually add milk. Cook, stirring
constantly, over low heat until
thickened. Add spaghetti, turkey,
½ cup cheese, mushrooms and
pimento; mix lightly. Spoon into
2-quart casserole. Toss bread cubes
with margarine and remaining
cheese; top casserole. Bake at 350°,
30 minutes or until lightly
browned. Makes 6 servings.

Preparation time: 30 minutes

Baking time: 30 minutes

Make ahead: Prepare as directed
except for topping with bread cubes
and baking. Cover; chill. When
ready to bake, toss bread cubes
with margarine and remaining
cheese. Top casserole; cover with
foil. Bake at 350°, 25 minutes.
Uncover; continue baking 30
minutes or until lightly browned.

MICROWAVE: Reduce margarine to
2 tablespoons. Microwave
margarine in 2-quart microwave-
safe casserole on High 30 seconds
or until melted. Add bread cubes;
toss. Microwave on High 3½ to 4½
minutes or until crisp, stirring
after 2 minutes. Remove from
casserole; set aside. Combine salad
dressing, flour and seasonings in
same casserole; gradually add
milk. Microwave on High 5 to 6
minutes or until thickened,
stirring after each minute. Stir in
spaghetti, turkey, ½ cup cheese,
mushrooms and pimento; mix
lightly. Cover; microwave on High
8 to 10 minutes or until thoroughly
heated, stirring after 5 minutes.
Stir; top with bread cubes. Sprinkle
with remaining cheese. Let stand 5
minutes.

Zesty Reuben Sandwiches

    MIRACLE WHIP Salad Dressing
1 tablespoon chili sauce
1⅓ cups shredded cabbage
1 cup (4 ozs.) shredded 100%
    Natural KRAFT Swiss
    Cheese
12 rye or pumpernickel bread
    slices
¾ lb. corned beef slices

Combine ¼ cup salad dressing and
chili sauce; mix well. Add cabbage
and cheese; mix lightly. For each
sandwich, cover one bread slice
with cabbage mixture; top with
corned beef and second bread slice.
Spread sandwich with salad
dressing. Grill until lightly
browned on both sides. Makes 6
sandwiches.

Preparation time: 10 minutes

Grilling time: 5 minutes

Hacienda Eggs

6 eggs, beaten
½ cup MIRACLE WHIP Salad Dressing
Salsa
2 cups corn chips
½ cup chopped green pepper

Combine eggs, salad dressing and ¼ cup salsa; mix well. Stir in chips and peppers. Pour into greased 9-inch pie plate. Bake at 350°, 20 minutes or until knife inserted in center comes out clean. Serve with sour cream and additional salsa. Top with additional chips, if desired. Makes 6 servings.

Preparation time: 10 minutes

Baking time: 20 minutes

MICROWAVE: Combine ingredients except chips in 1-quart microwave-safe measure or bowl; mix until well blended using wire whisk. Microwave on High 2 minutes, stirring after 1 minute. Stir in chips; pour into greased transparent 9-inch microwave-safe pie plate. Cover with plastic wrap; vent. Microwave on Medium (50%) 9 to 10 minutes or until egg mixture is almost set on bottom. (Lift pie plate to see bottom.) Let stand, covered, 2 minutes. Serve as directed.

Cheesy Corn Frittata

1½ cups cooked rice
¼ lb. VELVEETA Pasteurized Process Cheese Spread, sliced
3 eggs, beaten
1 8¾-oz. can cream style corn
½ cup chopped ham
⅓ cup MIRACLE WHIP Salad Dressing
Dash of pepper

Place rice in 10×6-inch baking dish. Top with process cheese spread. Combine remaining ingredients; pour over process cheese spread. Bake at 350°, 30 minutes. Top with additional process cheese spread, sliced, if desired. Let stand 5 minutes before serving. Makes 4 to 6 servings.

Preparation time: 25 minutes

Baking time: 30 minutes plus standing

Make ahead: Prepare recipe as directed except for baking; cover. Refrigerate up to 4 hours. When ready to serve, remove cover. Bake at 350°, 45 minutes. Continue as directed.

MICROWAVE: In 1-quart microwave-safe measure, combine eggs, corn, ham, salad dressing and pepper. Microwave on High 2 minutes, stirring after each minute. Using 10×6-inch microwave-safe dish, assemble recipe as directed. Cover with plastic wrap; vent. Microwave on High 7 to 9 minutes or until almost set, turning dish every 3 minutes. Top with additional process cheese spread, sliced, if desired. Let stand, covered, 5 minutes before serving.

Side Dishes

This chapter has a potpourri of creative cooking ideas, ranging from soups, vegetables and salad dressings to desserts. Add a special flair to an otherwise everyday meal with one of these fabulous recipes. Pictured here is Italian Grilled Vegetables; see page 80 for recipe

Italian Grilled Vegetables

½ cup MIRACLE WHIP Salad Dressing
½ cup KRAFT "Zesty" Italian Dressing
2 zucchini, cut in half lengthwise
2 summer squash, cut in half lengthwise
2 red, green or yellow peppers, cut into quarters

Combine dressings, mixing until well blended. Lightly score cut sides of vegetables; brush one side with salad dressing mixture. Place vegetables, salad dressing side up, on rack of broiler pan. Broil, 4 inches from heat source, 6 minutes. Turn; brush with salad dressing mixture. Continue broiling 6 minutes or until vegetables are tender. Serve with remaining salad dressing mixture. Makes 4 to 6 servings.

Preparation time: 10 minutes

Broiling time: 15 minutes

Variation: Substitute MIRACLE WHIP Light Reduced Calorie Salad Dressing with no cholesterol for Regular Salad Dressing.

Easy Carrot Cake

1 two-layer yellow cake mix
1¼ cups MIRACLE WHIP Salad Dressing
4 eggs
¼ cup cold water
2 teaspoons ground cinnamon
2 cups finely shredded carrots
½ cup chopped walnuts
Vanilla "Philly" Frosting (recipe follows)

In large bowl of electric mixer, combine cake mix, salad dressing, eggs, water and cinnamon, mixing at medium speed until well blended. Stir in carrots and walnuts. Pour into greased 13×9-inch baking pan. Bake 350°, 35 minutes or until wooden pick inserted in center comes out clean. Cool. Frost with Vanilla "Philly" Frosting. Makes 10 to 12 servings.

Preparation time: 25 minutes

Baking time: 35 minutes plus cooling

Vanilla "Philly" Frosting

1 3-oz. pkg. PHILADELPHIA BRAND Cream Cheese, softened
1 tablespoon milk
½ teaspoon vanilla
3 cups sifted powdered sugar

Combine cream cheese, milk and vanilla, mixing until well blended. Gradually add sugar, beating until light and fluffy.

Easy Carrot Cake with Vanilla "Philly" Frosting

Savory Corn Muffins

1 egg, beaten
3/4 cup MIRACLE WHIP Salad
  Dressing
1 4-oz. can chopped green
  chilies, drained
1 8 1/2-oz. pkg. corn muffin mix

Combine egg, salad dressing and chilies, mixing until well blended. Add muffin mix, mixing just until moistened. Spoon into greased medium-size muffin pan, filling each cup 2/3 full. Bake at 400°, 15 minutes. Loosen edge of muffins; remove from pan. Makes 1 dozen.

Preparation time: 10 minutes

Baking time: 15 minutes

Potato Soup with Cheese Crust

4 stalks celery, cut into 2-inch
  pieces
2 carrots, cut into 2-inch pieces
1 medium potato, peeled, cubed
1 onion, quartered
1 small turnip, peeled, quartered
2 1/3 cups cold water
1 13 3/4-oz. can chicken broth
1/4 teaspoon black pepper
3/4 cup MIRACLE WHIP Salad
  Dressing
1/4 teaspoon hot pepper sauce
1 cup (4 ozs.) 100% Natural
  KRAFT Shredded Sharp
  Cheddar Cheese
6 slices French or Italian bread,
  toasted

In food processor work bowl, place celery, carrots, potatoes, onions and turnips; process until vegetables are finely chopped. Spoon vegetable mixture into large saucepan. Add water, broth and pepper. Bring to boil; reduce heat. Simmer 15 minutes, stirring occasionally. Combine 1/4 cup salad dressing and hot pepper sauce. Gradually add salad dressing mixture to hot soup, using wire whisk to blend. Reduce heat to low. Combine remaining salad dressing and 1/2 cup cheese; spread onto toast. Spoon soup into ovenproof bowls; top with toast, cheese side up. Sprinkle with remaining cheese. Broil until golden brown and bubbling hot. Serve immediately. Makes six 1-cup servings.

Preparation time: 30 minutes

Broiling time: 5 minutes

Poppy Seed Dressing

1/2 cup MIRACLE WHIP Salad
  Dressing
2 tablespoons orange juice
1 tablespoon honey
1 teaspoon grated onion
1 teaspoon poppy seed

Combine ingredients, mixing until well blended. Cover; chill. Makes 3/4 cup.

Preparation time: 5 minutes plus chilling

Variation: Substitute MIRACLE WHIP Light Reduced Calorie Salad Dressing with no cholesterol for Regular Salad Dressing.

Blueberry Ice

1 envelope unflavored gelatin
3/4 cup cold water
1/2 cup MIRACLE WHIP Salad
　　Dressing
3/4 teaspoon grated lemon peel
3 cups blueberries
3/4 cup sugar

Combine gelatin and water in small saucepan; let stand 1 minute. Stir over low heat until dissolved. Cool. Combine salad dressing and peel; gradually add gelatin, mixing until well blended. Place blueberries in food processor work bowl; process 2 to 3 minutes or until pureed, scraping sides of work bowl as necessary. Add sugar and gelatin mixture; process 2 to 3 minutes or until light and foamy. Pour into 8-inch square baking pan; cover tightly. Freeze until firm. Place in refrigerator 15 minutes before serving. Spoon or scoop into serving dish. Makes 12 servings.

Preparation time: 25 minutes plus freezing

Variations: Omit lemon peel. Substitute 20-oz. pkg. frozen whole strawberries for blueberries.

Substitute MIRACLE WHIP Light Reduced Calorie Salad Dressing with no cholesterol for Regular Salad Dressing.

Fruity Ice Cream Dessert

3/4 cup MIRACLE WHIP Salad
　　Dressing
1 cup graham cracker crumbs
1 qt. vanilla ice cream, softened
3/4 cup dried mixed fruit
1/4 cup chopped pecans

Combine 1/4 cup salad dressing and crumbs, mixing until well blended. Press onto bottom of 9-inch springform pan. Bake at 350°, 5 minutes. Cool. Combine ice cream, remaining salad dressing, 1/2 cup fruit and pecans; mix well. Spoon over crust. Freeze until firm. Sprinkle with remaining fruit just before serving. Serve in wedges. Makes 10 to 12 servings.

Preparation time: 35 minutes plus freezing

Variation: Substitute 8 or 9-inch square pan for springform pan.

Microwave tip: To soften ice cream, microwave on Medium (50%) 40 seconds, stirring after 20 seconds.

Squash Soup

1 13¾-oz. can chicken broth
1 12-oz. pkg. frozen cooked
    winter squash
1 cup carrot slices
⅓ cup chopped onion
¼ teaspoon dried basil leaves,
    crushed
¾ cup MIRACLE WHIP Salad
    Dressing
1 tablespoon milk

Combine ingredients except salad dressing and milk in medium saucepan. Bring to boil. Reduce heat to medium. Cover; simmer 12 to 15 minutes or until carrots and onions are tender. Stir in ½ cup salad dressing, using wire whisk. Heat thoroughly, stirring occasionally. Combine remaining salad dressing and milk. Spoon soup into serving bowls; top with salad dressing mixture. Swirl gently with spoon. Makes four 1-cup servings.

Preparation time: 30 minutes

MICROWAVE: Substitute one acorn squash for frozen squash. Pierce squash several times with a fork. Microwave whole squash on High 2 minutes. Cut squash in half lengthwise; remove seeds. Place squash, cut side up, in shallow microwave-safe baking dish. Cover with plastic wrap; vent. Microwave on High 8 to 10 minutes or until fork-tender, turning dish every 4 minutes. Let stand 5 minutes. Scoop out squash; mash. Continue as directed.

Cajun Potato Topping

½ cup MIRACLE WHIP Salad
    Dressing
½ cup sour cream
¼ cup chopped celery
¼ cup chopped onion
¼ cup chopped green pepper
¼ teaspoon garlic powder
¼ teaspoon ground red pepper
¼ teaspoon ground cumin

Combine ingredients; mix well. Cover; chill. Serve over hot baked potatoes. Makes 1½ cups.

Preparation time: 10 minutes plus chilling

Wild Rice Extravaganza

1 6-oz. pkg. long-grain and wild
    rice
1 4-oz. can mushrooms, drained
⅓ cup MIRACLE WHIP Salad
    Dressing

Prepare rice as directed on package, omitting margarine. Add mushrooms and salad dressing during last 5 minutes of cooking. Let stand 5 minutes before serving. Makes 6 servings.

Preparation time: 30 minutes plus standing

Squash Soup

Spinach Bake

2 eggs, beaten
3/4 cup MIRACLE WHIP Salad Dressing
2 10-oz. pkgs. frozen chopped spinach, thawed, well drained
1 14-oz. can artichoke hearts, drained, cut into quarters
1/2 cup sour cream
1/4 cup (1 oz.) KRAFT 100% Grated Parmesan Cheese
6 crisply cooked bacon slices, crumbled

Combine eggs and 1/2 cup salad dressing, mixing until well blended. Add spinach and artichokes; mix lightly. Spoon mixture into lightly greased 10×6-inch baking dish. Combine remaining salad dressing, sour cream and cheese; mix well. Spoon over spinach mixture. Bake at 350°, 30 minutes or until set. Sprinkle with bacon. Makes 8 servings.

Preparation time: 10 minutes

Baking time: 30 minutes

MICROWAVE: Substitute 1½-quart microwave-safe casserole for 10×6-inch baking dish. Combine eggs and 1/2 cup salad dressing in casserole, mixing until well blended. Add spinach and artichokes; mix lightly. Microwave on High 8 to 9 minutes or until thoroughly heated, stirring every 3 minutes. Combine remaining salad dressing, sour cream and cheese; mix well. Spoon over spinach mixture. Microwave on High 1½ to 2 minutes or until sour cream mixture is warmed. (Do not over cook.) Sprinkle with bacon. Let stand 5 minutes.

Microwave tip: To thaw spinach, place frozen spinach in 1½-quart microwave-safe casserole; cover. Microwave on High 5 minutes. Break apart with fork; drain well.

Parmesan Potato Crisp

1/2 cup MIRACLE WHIP Salad Dressing
5 cups thin unpeeled potato slices
3/4 cup (3 ozs.) KRAFT 100% Grated Parmesan Cheese
Pepper (optional)

Generously brush 9-inch pie plate with salad dressing. Dry potato slices on paper towel. Arrange one layer of potatoes, edges slightly overlapping, on bottom of pie plate. Brush generously with salad dressing; sprinkle generously with cheese. Repeat layers, sprinkling occasionally with pepper. Bake at 400°, 30 minutes. Cover with foil; continue baking 30 minutes or until potatoes are tender. Immediately invert onto serving plate. Cut into wedges to serve. Makes 6 servings.

Preparation time: 10 minutes

Baking time: 1 hour

Variation: Substitute MIRACLE WHIP Light Reduced Calorie Salad Dressing with no cholesterol for Regular Salad Dressing.

Cucumber Dressing

1 cup MIRACLE WHIP Salad Dressing
½ cup shredded cucumber, drained, chopped
⅓ cup milk
2 tablespoons chopped parsley
¼ teaspoon pepper

Combine ingredients; mix well. Cover; chill. Makes 1½ cups.

Preparation time: 10 minutes plus chilling

Variation: Substitute MIRACLE WHIP Light Reduced Calorie Salad Dressing with no cholesterol for Regular Salad Dressing.

Devilish Good Eggs

6 hard-cooked eggs
¼ cup MIRACLE WHIP Salad Dressing
1 teaspoon KRAFT Pure Prepared Mustard
⅛ teaspoon salt

Cut eggs in half. Remove yolks; mash. Blend in salad dressing, mustard and salt. Refill whites. Garnish with parsley and pimento strips, if desired. Makes 1 dozen.

Preparation time: 25 minutes

Variations: Add one or more of the following to egg yolk mixture: 1 tablespoon pickle relish, 3 crisply cooked bacon slices, crumbled, 2 teaspoons chopped chives.

Substitute MIRACLE WHIP Light Reduced Calorie Salad Dressing with no cholesterol for Regular Salad Dressing.

Garden Vegetables and Rice

¾ cup cut green beans
¾ cup thin carrot slices
3 tablespoons green onion slices
1 garlic clove, minced
1 tablespoon oil
1½ cups hot cooked rice
⅓ cup MIRACLE WHIP Salad Dressing
2 tablespoons soy sauce
1 tablespoon dry roasted shelled sunflower seeds (optional)

Stir-fry beans, carrots, onions and garlic in oil in large skillet or wok until crisp-tender. Reduce heat to medium. Add remaining ingredients except sunflower seeds; heat thoroughly, stirring occasionally. Sprinkle with sunflower seeds just before serving. Makes 4 servings.

Preparation time: 25 minutes

Cooking time: 10 minutes

Lemon Cream Dessert

2 cups vanilla wafer crumbs
1 cup MIRACLE WHIP Salad Dressing
1 12-oz. container (4½ cups) frozen whipped topping, thawed
1 6-oz. can frozen lemonade or limeade concentrate, softened

Combine crumbs and ½ cup salad dressing; mix well. Press mixture onto bottom of 8-inch square baking pan. Bake at 350°, 10 minutes. Cool. Combine remaining ingredients, mixing until well blended. Spoon over crust; cover tightly. Freeze until firm. Place in refrigerator 10 minutes before cutting into squares to serve. Garnish as desired. Makes 9 to 12 servings.

Preparation time: 20 minutes plus freezing

Variation: Substitute strawberry or peach daiquiri frozen concentrate mix for lemonade concentrate.

Black Pepper Dressing

½ cup MIRACLE WHIP Salad Dressing
½ cup buttermilk
¾ teaspoon freshly ground black pepper

Combine ingredients, mixing until well blended. Cover; chill. Makes 1 cup.

Preparation time: 5 minutes plus chilling

Golden Twice-Baked Potatoes

4 large baking potatoes, baked
1½ cups (6 ozs.) 100% Natural KRAFT Shredded Sharp Cheddar Cheese
⅓ cup MIRACLE WHIP Salad Dressing
¼ cup milk
2 tablespoons green onion slices
4 crisply cooked bacon slices, crumbled

Slice tops from potatoes; scoop out center, leaving ⅛-inch shell. Mash potatoes. Add 1 cup cheese, salad dressing and milk; beat until fluffy. Spoon into shells. Place on ungreased cookie sheet. Top with remaining cheese, onions and bacon. Bake at 350°, 15 minutes. Makes 4 servings.

Preparation time: 1 hour 20 minutes

Baking time: 15 minutes

MICROWAVE: Prepare filling and spoon into potatoes as directed. Place in 12×8-inch microwave-safe baking dish. Microwave on High 7 to 8 minutes or until thoroughly heated, turning dish after 4 minutes. Top with remaining cheese, onions and bacon. Microwave on High 1½ to 2 minutes or until cheese is melted.

Microwave tip: To cook potatoes, pierce and place on paper towel. Microwave on High 15 to 18 minutes or until tender, turning and rearranging potatoes after 8 minutes. Let stand 5 minutes.

Lemon Cream Dessert

Traditional Sage Stuffing

1 cup MIRACLE WHIP Salad Dressing
3/4 cup cold water
2 teaspoons poultry seasoning
2 teaspoons ground sage
1/2 teaspoon ground marjoram
1/4 cup PARKAY Margarine
1 cup chopped celery
1 cup chopped onion
1/2 cup chopped mushrooms
1 12-oz. bag unseasoned stuffing mix
6 crisply cooked bacon slices, crumbled

Combine salad dressing, water and seasonings; mix well. Set aside. Melt margarine. Add celery, onions and mushrooms; cook until tender. Combine vegetable mixture, stuffing mix and bacon; mix lightly. Stir in salad dressing mixture. Spoon into 3-quart casserole or 13×9-inch baking dish; cover. Bake at 350°, 30 minutes. Makes 6 cups.

Preparation time: 25 minutes

Baking time: 30 minutes

Variations: Substitute 2/3 cup apple juice for water.

Substitute 1½ teaspoons dried thyme leaves, crushed, for poultry seasoning.

Omit onions. Add ½ cup chopped apple and ⅓ cup chopped nuts to stuffing mixture just before baking.

MICROWAVE: Prepare salad dressing mixture as directed. Microwave margarine in 3-quart microwave-safe casserole on High 1 minute or until melted. Add vegetables; microwave on High 5 to 6 minutes or until tender, stirring after 3 minutes. Add salad dressing mixture, stuffing and bacon; mix lightly. Microwave on High 10 minutes or until thoroughly heated, stirring every 5 minutes.

Zesty Thousand Island Dressing

1 cup MIRACLE WHIP Salad Dressing
1/2 cup chopped celery
1/4 cup chopped green pepper
1/4 cup finely chopped onion
1/4 cup chili sauce
1 hard-cooked egg, chopped
1 teaspoon Worcestershire sauce

Combine ingredients; mix well. Cover; chill. Makes 2 cups.

Preparation time: 25 minutes plus chilling

Variation: Substitute MIRACLE WHIP Light Reduced Calorie Salad Dressing with no cholesterol for Regular Salad Dressing.

Tasty Vegetable Medley

1 10¾-oz. can condensed cream of mushroom soup
⅓ cup MIRACLE WHIP Salad Dressing
1 16-oz. bag frozen mixed vegetables, thawed, drained
1 2.8-oz. can French fried onions

Combine soup and salad dressing; mix well. Stir in vegetables and half of onions. Spoon into 1-quart casserole. Bake at 350°, 30 minutes or until thoroughly heated. Sprinkle with remaining onions; continue baking 5 minutes. Makes 5 servings.

Preparation time: 5 minutes

Baking time: 35 minutes

MICROWAVE: Substitute 1½-quart microwave-safe casserole for 1-quart casserole. Combine soup and salad dressing in 1½-quart microwave-safe casserole. Stir in vegetables and half of onions; cover. Microwave on High 7 to 8 minutes or until thoroughly heated, stirring after 4 minutes. Stir; sprinkle with remaining onions. Microwave, uncovered, on High 1 minute.

Make ahead: Prepare recipe as directed except for baking. Cover; chill. When ready to serve, remove cover. Bake at 350°, 30 minutes or until thoroughly heated. Continue as directed.

Microwave tip: To thaw vegetables, place in 1½-quart microwave-safe casserole; cover. Microwave on Medium (50%) 10 to 12 minutes or until thawed, stirring after 5 minutes.

Cucumber-Dill Potato Topping

½ cup MIRACLE WHIP Salad Dressing
½ cup plain yogurt
½ cup chopped cucumber
½ teaspoon dill weed

Combine ingredients; mix well. Cover; chill. Serve over hot baked potatoes. Makes 1⅓ cups.

Preparation time: 5 minutes plus chilling

Variation: Substitute MIRACLE WHIP Light Reduced Calorie Salad Dressing with no cholesterol for Regular Salad Dressing

Parmesan-Chive Potato Topping

½ cup MIRACLE WHIP Salad Dressing
½ cup sour cream
¼ cup (1 oz.) KRAFT 100% Grated Parmesan Cheese
1 teaspoon chopped chives

Combine ingredients; mix well. Cover; chill. Serve over hot baked potatoes. Makes 1 cup.

Preparation time: 5 minutes plus chilling

Variation: Substitute MIRACLE WHIP Light Reduced Calorie Salad Dressing with no cholesterol for Regular Salad Dressing and plain yogurt for sour cream.

Chewy Double Chocolate Brownies

    2 eggs, beaten
    ½ cup MIRACLE WHIP Salad
        Dressing
    ¼ cup cold water
    1 21.5-oz. pkg. fudge brownie
        mix
    1 6-oz. pkg. semi-sweet
        chocolate pieces

Combine eggs, salad dressing and water; mix well. Stir in brownie mix, mixing just until moistened. Add chocolate pieces; mix lightly. Pour into greased 13×9-inch baking pan. Bake at 350°, 30 minutes or until edges begin to pull away from sides of pan. Cool; sprinkle with sifted powdered sugar, if desired. Cut into squares. Makes approximately 2 dozen.

Preparation time: 5 minutes

Baking time: 30 minutes plus cooling

Lemony Fruit Topping

    ½ cup MIRACLE WHIP Light
        Reduced Calorie Salad
        Dressing with no cholesterol
    ½ cup lemon flavored yogurt

Combine ingredients; mix well. Cover; chill. Serve over fresh fruit. Makes 1 cup.

Preparation time: 5 minutes plus chilling.

Variation: Substitute MIRACLE WHIP Salad Dressing for Reduced Calorie Salad Dressing with no cholesterol.

Coleslaw Dressing

    ¼ cup milk
    ½ cup MIRACLE WHIP Salad
        Dressing
    1 tablespoon vinegar
    ½ teaspoon KRAFT Pure
        Prepared Mustard

Gradually add milk to salad dressing, mixing until blended. Stir in remaining ingredients. Makes ³/₄ cup.

Preparation time: 5 minutes

Variation: Substitute MIRACLE WHIP Light Reduced Calorie Salad Dressing with no cholesterol for Regular Salad Dressing.

Fruit Dip

    ½ cup MIRACLE WHIP Salad
        Dressing
    2 tablespoons KRAFT Apricot,
        Peach, Pineapple or Red
        Raspberry Preserves
    1 cup thawed frozen whipped
        topping

Combine salad dressing and preserves; mix well. Fold in whipped topping. Serve with assorted fruit dippers. Makes 1¹/₃ cups.

Preparation time: 5 minutes

Chewy Double Chocolate Brownies

Index

Almond-Chicken Casserole, 67
Appetizers (*see also* **Dips and spreads**)
    Artichoke Appetizers, 21
    Baked Potato Spears, 22
    Cheesy Crab Squares, 14
    Creamy Egg Rolls, 18
    Garden Appetizers, 22
    Garden Vegetable Party Pitas, 21
    Party Chicken Sandwiches, 17
    Southwestern Appetizer Torte, 9
    Turkey Empanadas, 18
    Vegetable-Laced Bagelettes, 10
    Vegetable Pizza, 9
Apricot Sauce, 18
Artichoke Appetizers, 21

Baked Chicken Parmesan, 61
Baked Potato Spears, 22
Beach Picnic Sandwiches, 63
Beef
    Zesty Reuben Sandwiches, 76
Black Pepper Dressing, 88
BLT Salad Toss, 33
Blueberry Ice, 83
Blue Cheese Salad, 26

Cajun Baked Fish, 75
Cajun Chicken Salad, 53
Cajun Potato Topping, 85
Carrot Salad, 29
Cheesy Corn Frittata, 77
Cheesy Crab Squares, 14
Chewy Double Chocolate Brownies, 93
Chicken (*see also* **Turkey**)
    Almond-Chicken Casserole, 67
    Baked Chicken Parmesan, 61
    Cajun Chicken Salad, 53
    Chicken Chutney Salad, 50
    Chicken Dijon, 69
    Country Chicken Bake, 70
    Layered Taco Salad, 54
    Party Chicken Sandwiches, 17
Cinnamon-Apple Coleslaw, 34
Coleslaw Dressing, 93
Country Chicken Bake, 70
Crabmeat
    Cheesy Crab Squares, 14
    Crab & Broccoli Frittata, 58
    Seafood Pasta Salad, 46
Cranberry Holiday Ring, 37

Cranberry Waldorf Fluff, 30
Creamy Dill Dip, 9
Creamy Egg Rolls, 18
Creamy Spinach Dip, 6
Crunchy Pea Salad, 30
Cucumber-Dill Potato Salad, 46
Cucumber-Dill Potato Topping, 91
Cucumber Dressing, 87

Desserts
    Blueberry Ice, 83
    Chewy Double Chocolate Brownies, 93
    Easy Carrot Cake, 80
    Fruity Ice Cream Dessert, 83
    Lemon Cream Dessert, 88
Devilish Good Eggs, 87
Dips and spreads
    Creamy Dill Dip, 9
    Creamy Spinach Dip, 6
    Fruit Dip, 93
    Guacamole, 54
    Guacamole Dip, 6
    Hearty Barbecue Dip, 22
    Hot Swiss and Almond Spread, 17
    Munching Onion Dip, 10
    Parma Dip, 22
    Pesto-Layered Spread, 6
    Shrimp Spread, 10
    Smooth Cheddar Spread, 10
    Sombrero Appetizer, 14

Easy Carrot Cake, 80
Easy Ham & Potatoes au Gratin, 68
Eggplant Rolls, 63
Eggs
    Cheesy Corn Frittata, 77
    Crab & Broccoli Frittata, 58
    Devilish Good Eggs, 87
    Hacienda Eggs, 77

Fettucini Italiano, 58
Fish
    Cajun Baked Fish, 75
    Nautical Salad, 53
    Tuna-Broccoli Casserole, 75
Frosting, Vanilla "Philly", 80
Fruit
    Blueberry Ice, 83
    Fruity Ice Cream Dessert, 83
    "Just for Kids" Sandwich, 64

Fruit Cloud, 37
Fruit Dip, 93
Fruit salads
    Cranberry Holiday Ring, 37
    Cranberry Waldorf Fluff, 30
    Fruit Cloud, 37
    Kids' Favorite Fruit Salad, 38
    Our Basic Waldorf Salad, 29
    Piña Colada Freeze, 30
    Potpourri Fruit Bowl, 26
    Raspberry-Lemon Gelatin Salad, 34
    Sun-Sational Lemon Mold, 33
    Walnut-Grape Salad, 33
Fruity Ice Cream Dessert, 83

Garden Appetizers, 22
Garden Salad, 38
Garden Vegetable Party Pitas, 21
Garden Vegetables and Rice, 87
Gelatin salads
    Cranberry Holiday Ring, 37
    Fruit Cloud, 37
    Raspberry-Lemon Gelatin Salad, 34
    Sun-Sational Lemon Mold, 33
Golden Twice-Baked Potatoes, 88
Great American Potato Salad, 45
Guacamole, 54
Guacamole Dip, 6
Gyros Sandwiches, 72

Hacienda Eggs, 77
Ham
    Easy Ham & Potatoes au Gratin, 68
    Ham & Pasta Salad, 53
    Stuffed Pasta Shells, 72
    Swiss Club Bundles, 61
    Zucchini Ham Bake, 62
Hearty Barbecue Dip, 22
Heavenly Seven-Layer Salad, 38
Honey-Mustard Coleslaw, 34
Hot Swiss and Almond Spread, 17

Italian Grilled Vegetables, 80
Italian Pasta Salad, 42

Jambalaya Salad, 54
"Just for Kids" Sandwich, 64

Kids' Favorite Fruit Salad, 38

Layered Taco Salad, 54
Lemon Cream Dessert, 88
Lemony Fruit Topping, 93

Main-dish salads
    Cajun Chicken Salad, 53
    Chicken Chutney Salad, 50
    Ham & Pasta Salad, 53
    Jambalaya Salad, 54

    Layered Taco Salad, 54
    Nautical Salad, 53
    Northwest Macaroni Salad, 50
    Pizza Lovers' Salad, 50
Meats (*see also* individual listings)
    Beach Picnic Sandwiches, 63
    Gyros Sandwiches, 72
Microwave Potato Salad, 46
Microwave recipes
    Almond-Chicken Casserole, 67
    Baked Chicken Parmesan, 61
    Cajun Baked Fish, 75
    Cheesy Corn Frittata, 77
    Chicken Dijon, 69
    Crab & Broccoli Frittata, 58
    Easy Ham & Potatoes au Gratin, 68
    Eggplant Rolls, 63
    Fettucini Italiano, 58
    Golden Twice-Baked Potatoes, 88
    Hacienda Eggs, 77
    Hot Swiss and Almond Spread, 17
    Microwave Potato Salad, 46
    Midwestern Stir-Fry, 67
    Oriental Pork, 62
    Parmesan Turkey Divan, 68
    Sombrero Appetizer, 14
    Spinach Bake, 86
    Squash Soup, 85
    Stuffed Pasta Shells, 72
    Tasty Vegetable Medley, 91
    Traditional Sage Stuffing, 90
    Tuna-Broccoli Casserole, 75
    Turkey Tetrazzini, 76
Midwestern Stir-Fry, 67
Muffins, Savory Corn, 82
Munching Onion Dip, 10
Mustard Sauce, 18

Nautical Salad, 53
Northwest Macaroni Salad, 50

One Pot Pasta Salad, 42
Oriental Pork, 62
Our Basic Waldorf Salad, 29

Parma Dip, 22
Parmesan-Chive Potato Topping, 91
Parmesan Potato Crisp, 86
Parmesan Turkey Divan, 68
Party Chicken Sandwiches, 17
Pasta
    Fettucini Italiano, 58
    Stuffed Pasta Shells, 72
Pasta salads
    Ham & Pasta Salad, 53
    Italian Pasta Salad, 42
    Northwest Macaroni Salad, 50
    One Pot Pasta Salad, 42
    Pesto Pasta Salad, 45

Pasta salads (*continued*)
  Seafood Pasta Salad, 46
  Summer Pasta Salad, 45
Pesto-Layered Spread, 6
Pesto Pasta Salad, 45
Piña Colada Freeze, 30
Pineapple-Bacon Coleslaw, 34
Pizza Lovers' Salad, 50
Poppy Seed Dressing, 82
Pork
  Midwestern Stir-Fry, 67
  Oriental Pork, 62
  Pork Piccata, 70
Potato Soup with Cheese Crust, 82
Potpourri Fruit Bowl, 26

Raspberry-Lemon Gelatin Salad, 34
Rice
  Garden Vegetables and Rice, 87
  Wild Rice & Pepper Salad, 26
  Wild Rice Extravaganza, 85

Salad dressings
  Black Pepper Dressing, 88
  Coleslaw Dressing, 93
  Cucumber Dressing, 87
  Poppy Seed Dressing, 82
  Zesty Thousand Island Dressing, 90
Salads (*see* individual listings)
Sauces
  Apricot Sauce, 18
  Mustard Sauce, 18
Savory Corn Muffins, 82
Seafood Pasta Salad, 46
Shrimp
  Jambalaya Salad, 54
  Shrimp Spread, 10
Smooth Cheddar Spread, 10
Sombrero Appetizer, 14
Soups
  Potato Soup with Cheese Crust, 82
  Squash Soup, 85
Southwestern Appetizer Torte, 9
Southwestern-Style Potato Salad, 42
Spinach Bake, 86
Spreads (*see* **Dips and spreads**)
Squash Soup, 85
Stuffed Pasta Shells, 72
Stuffing, Traditional Sage, 90
Summer Pasta Salad, 45
Sun-Sational Lemon Mold, 33
Swiss Club Bundles, 61

Tasty Turkey Pot Pie, 64
Tasty Vegetable Medley, 91
Toppings
  Cajun Potato Topping, 85
  Cucumber-Dill Potato Topping, 91
  Lemony Fruit Topping, 93
  Parmesan-Chive Potato Topping, 91

Traditional Coleslaw, 34
Traditional Sage Stuffing, 90
Tuna
  Nautical Salad, 53
  Tuna-Broccoli Casserole, 75
Turkey (*see also* **Chicken**)
  Parmesan Turkey Divan, 68
  Stuffed Pasta Shells, 72
  Tasty Turkey Pot Pie, 64
  Turkey Empanadas, 18
  Turkey Tetrazzini, 76

Vanilla "Philly" Frosting, 80
Vegetable-Laced Bagelettes, 10
Vegetable Pizza, 9
Vegetables
  Artichoke Appetizers, 21
  Baked Potato Spears, 22
  Cheesy Corn Frittata, 77
  Easy Ham & Potatoes au Gratin, 68
  Eggplant Rolls, 63
  Garden Appetizers, 22
  Garden Vegetables and Rice, 87
  Golden Twice-Baked Potatoes, 88
  Italian Grilled Vegetables, 80
  Parmesan Potato Crisp, 86
  Potato Soup with Cheese Crust, 82
  Spinach Bake, 86
  Squash Soup, 85
  Tasty Vegetable Medley, 91
  Zucchini Ham Bake, 62
Vegetable salads
  BLT Salad Toss, 33
  Blue Cheese Salad, 26
  Carrot Salad, 29
  Cinnamon-Apple Coleslaw, 34
  Crunchy Pea Salad, 30
  Cucumber-Dill Potato Salad, 46
  Garden Salad, 38
  Great American Potato Salad, 45
  Heavenly Seven-Layer Salad, 38
  Honey-Mustard Coleslaw, 34
  Microwave Potato Salad, 46
  Pineapple-Bacon Coleslaw, 34
  Pizza Lovers' Salad, 50
  Southwestern-Style Potato Salad, 42
  Traditional Coleslaw, 34
  Wild Rice & Pepper Salad, 26
  Zippy Bean Salad, 29

Walnut-Grape Salad, 33
Wild Rice & Pepper Salad, 26
Wild Rice Extravaganza, 85

Zesty Reuben Sandwiches, 76
Zesty Thousand Island Dressing, 90
Zippy Bean Salad, 29
Zucchini Ham Bake, 62